Author and Creative Director: Andrea Hungerford
Photographer and Editor: Karen DeWitz
Pattern Designers: Andrea Hungerford, Sloane Rosenthal
Models: Alia Cohn, Emmersen Cohn, Joanna Espine, Katie Porter
Patterns Technical Editor: Alexandra Viegel
Marketing and Social Media: Hannah Thiessen
Map Artist: Peggy Dean
Printer: Cenveo

ORDERING INFORMATION
By Hand is published three times annually. Subscriptions or single-issue
purchases can be ordered online at: www.byhandserial.com.

Wholesale inquiries may be submitted via e-mail to www.nnkpress.com.

Published by Blueberry Hill
www.byhandserial.com
info@byhandserial.com

PRINTED IN THE USA
This book is printed on Forest Stewardship Council certified paper.
FSC certification ensures that the paper in this publication contains
fibers from well managed and responsibly harvested forests that meet
strict environmental and socioeconomic standards.

FIRST EDITION
Spring 2017

By Hand

making communities

Lookbook No. 3: Nashville

Table Of Contents

Nashville

The city of Nashville is a juxtaposition of old and new. You see it everywhere: in the modern skyscrapers rising up next to Ryman Auditorium and Union Station; in the new residents (many recently relocated from other parts of the country) whose neighbors have southern roots that they can trace back for generations; and even in the many murals, where homages to the Nashville of old like "Acme Feed & Seed" coexist with "Make Music Not War" and the neon signs that light up Broadway.

This interplay between honoring tradition and celebrating new ideas and ingenuity can be found in the creative side of Nashville, as well. Many of the makers I interviewed are exploring fresh approaches to crafts and skills that are steeped in history. Katie Gonzalez of Linen Laid Felt is an artist working with paper and printmaking—both of which have deep historical roots in Nashville, where the oldest printing press in the country still operates. Music City Leather's custom bootmaker, Wes Shugart, uses skills and techniques in custom making cowboy boots that have been honed for generations, in a craft that owes its very existence to American history. Denton Hunker of Hunker Bag Co. works with leather and canvas—materials long used by craftspeople—to create utilitarian bags such as duffels that are also functional art because of their beauty and the care that has gone into crafting them. Other makers in this book similarly give a fresh new take to traditional hand crafts such as spinning and dyeing fiber with natural materials.

The wonder and beauty of what these artists create is found where the old meets the new—where traditional hand crafts are given a modern interpretation or a fresh approach that makes us look at them in a new light. Beauty also shines where traditional crafts are revitalized so that new generations can appreciate the skill and painstaking work that goes into the creation of such fundamental pieces as books and bags, boots and yarn. Nashville is a fascinating place—with one foot firmly in southern tradition and the other foot anxious to step ahead into the future—to watch how this seeming contradiction manifests itself in art and in the creation of new ways of thinking.

Making Communities

Whenever I'm chatting with a group of knitters, sooner or later someone asks **the question**: "Are you a process knitter or a product knitter?" These two categories seem to divide the knitting world - those of us who knit for the joy of the activity itself, the feel of the needles moving and the yarn turning into fabric beneath our fingers - and those of us who knit for the final result, a garment or accessory that we created and can now use.

Process knitters don't gasp at the idea of frogging; they are blase about UFOs (unfinished objects) lingering in their project bags for months (if not years) on end; and they seem to enjoy horrifying other knitters with tales of completed sweaters ripped out again and again, just to get the fit right or to use the yarn all over again for something else.

Product knitters, on the other hand, share war stories about the size of their queues, they compare sweater completion rates, and they sympathize over the siren call of a constant stream of new patterns, pushing the knitter to quick, finish up what's on the needles now, so the next project can begin.

I usually confess to being a product knitter - I say confess, because there is a feeling of guilt that goes along with the label. As if it is shameful that the mere act of knitting itself isn't enough - that the fact that I want the finished item somehow cheapens or demeans the making process. However, I've recently decided to claim

both of these titles. Of course I am a process knitter- if I didn't love the act of knitting, I could certainly find handknit sweaters to buy, or friends who would knit for me. There are so many things about the process of knitting that enthrall me - the infinite variety of colors, how texture can change the feel and appearance of the fabric I'm creating, the different - yet all wonderful - qualities of the many kinds of animal and plant fibers that make up yarn. And, perhaps most important, the meditative quality that knitting brings to me - how the repetitive rhythm and the movement of my hands slows my heartrate and frees my mind to wander (unless I'm struggling with a complicated cable pattern, that is!)

But all of this doesn't change the fact that I knit to create a finished object, and that much of the reason I knit is to be able to use the functional art that I have created. I love the feeling of that last cast-off, taking the finished item off the needles, and trying it on for the first time. I love the excitement of deciding on the next project, purusing all of my options for the next yarn purchase, planning out the colors I will use. For me, the end result is equally as important as the journey that got me there.

I think that most of the things we create with our hands also combine process and product in equal parts. Gardening, for instance, is certainly about the harvest, but it's also about the peace and joy it brings us to place the seedlings in the soil, to nuture the plants as they grow, and even the meditative quality that weeding can bring on a warm summer morning. Making jam is as much about each of the steps - picking the berries, washing and cooking them, carefully ladling the finished jam into jars and gently lowering them into the hot bath canner - as it is about seeing all of those jewel-toned jars stacked neatly in the pantry.

I talk with folks a lot about the importance of preserving the skills of hand making, and passing these down to the next generation, but I think that it is just as important to pass down the reverence and love of the process. I worry that in today's fast-paced world, where everything is at our fingertips and we expect instanteous results, younger generations won't come to understand the gifts that an appreciation of the process of making can bring.

Many of the stories shared in Lookbook No. 3 highlight this balance between process and product, and the makers' love for both ends of this spectrum. These makers - and the thousands of others like them who see value in both process and product - give me hope that these important lessons will continue to be learned, so long as there are people out there who continue to be interested in making by hand.

Warmly,
Andrea

In addition to Craft South, the 12th Avenue South neighborhood has a wonderful array of dining and shopping options, including Imogene + Willie custom-made denim, housed in an old converted garage with all of the paper patterns hanging from the rafters (below), the Frothy Monkey coffeehouse in a house with a wide front porch perfect for summer sitting and sipping (top), and Amelia's Flower Truck, often found parked in front of Imogene + Willie (middle).

Mecca for Makers: Craft South and Anna Maria Horner

Craft South is a mecca for the multi-crafter, or for makers who are eager to try their hand at another form of functional art. The shop itself is chock full of supplies and inspiration for quilting, apparel sewing, embroidery, crewel, knitting, weaving, rug tying . . . you name a fiber or fabric art form, and it's likely that you can find the supplies and the notions you need waiting for you here. Hand dyed yards of fabric from as far away as Australia share the shelves with locally spun yarns and a carefully curated selection of treasures hand made by local artists and craftspeople.

The founder and owner of Craft South, Anna Maria Horner, has a long history in both Tennessee and in crafting. Raised in East Tennessee, she was surrounded by a mother, aunts, and grandmothers who were always sewing, embroidering, or making something. She earned a fine arts degree and then opened a clothing shop with her mom right out of college. She quickly moved on to freelance product design for other companies, and was approached by Free Spirit fabrics to design her first fabric collection in 2006. By that point, sewing had taken a back burner to her other design pursuits, but "designing fabric by the yard moved me back into sewing and piqued my interest in quilting. I became interested in providing makers with supplies and beautiful materials, instead of hand making things for sale myself." She taught herself to quilt over time, and "every quilt I made the first four or five years of designing quilting fabrics was a process of me educating myself. Only in the past handful of years do I feel like I've learned enough about all of the variations of putting quilt tops together in ways that save time and efficiently use materials."

happiness is handmade

Since that time, Anna Maria has continued product design for fabric and ribbon, as well as becoming a spokesperson for Janome Sewing Machines. She is also a published author of several hand crafting books, including a needlework book and a book on sewing baby projects. She explains that Craft South grew out of a desire for a home base from which to teach other makers. "As my business with fabrics grew, so did requests for teaching . . . I found that when I traveled to teach, the students were also traveling to take the classes. It was a challenge to accept teaching invitations as my family grew, and I love to teach and the engagement with my students that it creates. I had an online business that had been run out of my house, so Craft South created a brick and mortar location for that business, along with room to teach." And Nashville was the perfect place for the new store. "For as big as it is, Nashville was light on craft supplies, and this was a perfect opportunity to provide that for the city." Craft South opened in May 2015 and immediately began hosting both regular classes and guest instructors from all over the world.

Anna Maria articulates the focus of Craft South as "the trinity of craft: patchwork, sewing, and embroidery." The store stocks 400+ colors of embroidery floss and 400+ colors of crewel wool yarn. The big, bright space is also a Janome sewing machine dealership and has studio space for classes and workshops. "I am really interested in all crafts, so I stocked this place just how I might stock my dream studio." Many of Craft South's clients are cross-crafters—those who already know a hand skill and are interested in learning others. "My goal is that our format supports people who are already interested in craft, such as the quilter who decides to become a knitter."

Craft South uses several different structures for its classes. There are typically 2-3 day intensive weekend workshops held every month, when a notable designer comes into town as a guest teacher. "Those events inspired us to choose this neighborhood, where there is so much within walking distance—coffee, wine bars, B&Bs—it's a great place to visit. Most people travel in from out of town for these classes, and we wanted the whole experience to be really pleasurable for anyone who spends that time with us." The store also hosts a variety of regular classes month to month: patchwork, beginning garment sewing, knitting, weaving, series that are specific to kids, sewing machine introduction classes, and private lessons for starting and finishing a project, among others. Anna Maria notes that beginning garment sewing classes are very popular, as are beginning knitting and weaving.

While Anna Maria spearheads the store, her full-time job is as a pattern designer, fabric designer, and Janome representative. She gives credit to the "fantastic team" she has in place at Craft South that allows her to pursue her other endeavors, all while she and her husband raise their seven children, ages 3 to 25. In recent years, Anna Maria has launched the wildly popular Loominous and Loominous 2 collections, as well as fabric lines in voile, velveteen, and other materials. The Loominous collections are yarn dyed, which means that instead of starting as a solid white piece of cloth with colors and a pattern printed on one side, the design you see in the cloth is created by dyed threads that are woven in a pattern. "In designing my print collections, I like them to feel like they were collected over time." Anna Maria has designed patterns

Craft South

Address: 2516 12th Ave. South, Nashville

Phone: 615.928.8766

Website: www.craft-south.com

Products: Patchwork and sewing, embroidery, knitting and crochet, patterns and kits, Janome sewing machines, Handcrafted South products and gifts

Classes: Weaving, knitting, garment sewing, rug twine weaving, patchwork, accessories sewing, kids crafts, and more

for quilts, garments, and accessories, and is in the process of developing a new line of sewing patterns called Simple Start, which are "really at the beginning of garment sewing, meant to be skill-building from one project to the next, based on workshops and classes we teach here. Everything I do here at Craft South either validates or informs what I'm doing as a fabric and pattern designer. As a shop owner, I now have the benefit of being the person I've been selling my fabric lines to all these years. I have a better understanding of what shops are looking for and need."

Craft South's Nashville location means that it plays a role in a vibrant, ever-changing creative community. Anna Maria notes that there is an history of self-reliance and hand making in the south, and that history is now overlaid by the creative growth the city is experiencing. "I've watched the city grow from a mid-size southern town to a real diverse metropolis. Music provides a special undercurrent, and there are so many people moving here from all over the country for work in television, music, video production, even fashion." Craft South plays an integral role in supporting creative ventures for makers of all kinds, and by helping makers expand their skills and learn new ones. ⌘

Nashville offers a surprising variety of impressive street art. Some murals have become so well known that they are identifers for particular neighborhoods, and having your photograph taken next to these works of art has become an item on many visitors' to-do lists.

9

Jammers

by Andrea Hungerford

When I give a handmade gift, so much effort has gone into creating it that I want the gift's presentation to be just as thoughtful. It's important to me that not only the gift itself, but also the way it is given, reflects the care and attention that handcrafting represents. For some reason, this can be the hardest part; I put all of the work into creating a beautiful gift by hand, but then when it comes to how to wrap it for gift giving, it's like I run out of inspiration, or time, or energy, and I end up just slapping something together.

My homemade jam is the perfect example of this gift giving quandary. For years, I have made jams from start to finish – grown the berries, picked and washed them, cooked them into jam, and then hot bath canned them so that they'll last well into the winter. This process can take days, and oftentimes a huge number of berries is reduced to just a very few jars of jam, making each one worth its weight in gold (or at least my aching back and berry juice-stained fingers!) But when it comes to giving out these precious half-pints, I've never been able to find a way to reflect all that went into making them. I tell myself that I'll find the perfect little box to buy, and a little something to make the perfect gift giving set, but in the end, more often than not I end up unceremoniously handing the jar to the intended recipient without the fanfare it deserves.

Recently, I was thinking about the upcoming fruit season as spring turns into summer, and taking inventory of what jams remain in my pantry. Will I put up marionberry jam this year? Will it be a bumper blackberry crop? Do I have the patience to make sweet cherry preserves this year – oh, all those pits! These ruminations led me to consider my oft-repeated gift giving dilemma – and that, in turn, led to my creation of the jammer.

Designed as a jam cozy or caddy, the jammer is perfectly sized for gifting two half-pint jars of jam or jelly. I've chosen the fabrics and interfacing specifically to give the sides of the jammer enough stability to hold jelly jars upright, and the leather handles are specified at a length and width that makes it easy to hold and carry the jammer.

When gifting your jams, cozy them up in the jammer with leftover scraps of the fabric you used, or shredded paper or tissue paper so that they don't knock together. And if you want to make your gift extra special, pair a jar of homemade jam with these adorably perfect jam pots, made exclusively for *By Hand Serial* by the talented duo at JaMpdx. Hand-thrown in porcelain clay and then painstakingly decorated, down to the strawberry handle lid and the miniature ceramic spoon, the jam pot and a jar of your homemade best, all stylishly packaged in a jammer, will make a stunning gift! (JaMpdx jam pots are available on *By Hand Serial's* website.)

Materials:
* Fat quarter or ¼ yard of outer fabric
* Fat quarter or ¼ yard of inner fabric
* ¼ yard firm fusible interfacing (I used Pellon 809 Décor-Bond(R))
* Two ¾" wide, 7" long leather straps
* 4 metal rivets and a rivet setting tool
* An awl, or nail and hammer
* Matching thread

You can experiment with which fabrics you like — I found the best combination to be a cotton fabric and a canvas fabric. It doesn't matter which you use

on the inside and which on the outside of the jammer – try it both ways and see which you like best. You can also personalize your jammer with embroidery. Try a simple embroidered raspberry, strawberry, or cherry, depending on what type of jam you're giving. For these jammers, I used the following cotton fabrics: Lecien Dots, Kiyohara small gingham, Robert Kaufman Essex Yarn Dyed, and Robert Kaufman Sevenberry Petite. The canvas is organic cotton duck canvas in red. This is the ideal project to customize to whichever kind of jam you're giving, or to help empty out that fabric stash!

Both the leather straps and the rivets are sourced from Etsy. Make sure you get a rivet installing kit, as well; it is very low tech, but also very helpful.

Seam allowances are ½" unless otherwise specified.

1. Cut two 7" x 10" rectangles each from outer fabric, inner fabric, and craft interfacing.

2. Fuse the interfacing to the wrong sides of the outer fabric pieces, following package directions.

3. Place the interfaced outer fabric pieces right sides together and sew around the two short sides and one long side, pivoting at the corners. Press seams open.

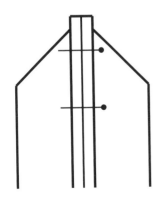

Figure 1

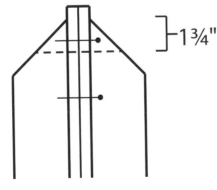

1¾"

Figure 2

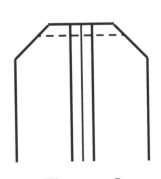

Figure 3

4. Box the bottom corners: With piece inside out, fold so the long bottom seam sits directly on top of a short side seam and pin to keep the layers from shifting (Fig. 1). Measure 1 3/4" from the point, draw a light guideline across in pencil, then stitch along the line (Fig. 2). Trim the point off leaving a 1/2" seam allowance (Fig. 3). Repeat for other side. Turn the piece right side out, fold and press to form bottom and side creases.

5. Repeat steps 3 and 4 with the inner fabric but leave the piece inside out, and press the creases in as if the piece will remain inside out.

6. Fold the top edge of the outer box 3/4" to the wrong side and press. Fold the top edge of the inner box 1/2" to the wrong side and press.

6. Drop the inner box into the outer box, wrong sides facing each other. Match at the side seams and creases and pin, then pin all around the top edge, accommodating for any slight difference in size between the two pieces by carefully stretching or contracting the outer and inner sides so that they line up nicely. Pin the fabrics so that approximately 1/4" of the inner box shows above the edge of the outer box to create a nice rim of contrasting fabric. Stitch around the top, close to the edge of the outer box.

7. Fold the finished jammer along the four bottom edges and the four side edges; iron in creases and corners to give the jammer a clean, finished look. Take your time with this step – the better defined the creases and edges are, the better your jammer will hold up to repeated use.

8. Using a hammer and nail or an awl, poke a hole in the center of each leather strap ¼" from each end. Then hold the strap against the short side of the jammer so that the strap's short edges are ¾" down from the top edge of the jammer and 1/4" in from the corner (or center the straps however you'd like on the jammer's short ends). Insert a pen into the holes in the leather strap, so that you make two corresponding marks on the short side of the jammer. Using an X-Acto knife or other sharp tool, make a small cut or hole in the jammer at each mark. Install one rivet into each of the four fabric and leather holes, following the instructions on the rivet kit.

Feel free to experiment with different fabrics and embellishments to reflect whatever unique goodie you will be tucking into your jammer. Happy gifting!

Recipe: Whiskey Raspberry Jam

by Jenn Davis-Baldwin

INGREDIENTS
8 cups Raspberries - fresh or frozen
6 cups Sugar
6 tablespoons Meyer Lemon juice - fresh squeezed
1/3 cup Chambord
1/2 cup Whiskey
1/3-1/2 cup Classic Real Fruit Pectin

DIRECTIONS
Start by placing a saucer with 4 metal spoons in the freezer on a flat surface for testing of the jams later.

Combine berries, sugar and lemon juice in a large stainless steel or enamel saucepan.
Heat mixture at a medium high to high heat to dissolve all sugar.
Once heating, it may start bubbling or foaming. Foaming indicates that the pot is too hot, and the moisture is being absorbed. Reduce the heat to decrease the foaming in the center of the pot, allowing it to form on the sides.
Stir frequently to prevent sticking.

You may find the jam to be lumpy from the whole berries; at any time, use a masher to crush the fruit into desired thickness. I personally use an immersion blender, because I prefer the silkiness it achieves; this helps to open the seeds and to break them down a little more.

Once your berries are at the desired texture, add 1/3 cup pectin, Chambord and whiskey. Stir on high heat for 5 minutes.

To test doneness, reduce heat and use a test spoon from the freezer to determine the thickness you're wanting to achieve. Return spoon with jam on it back into the freezer for 2-4 min, then tilt the spoon vertically to see whether the jam runs. If it runs, add a little more pectin, cook on medium heat for another 5-11 minutes, and retest with another spoon. If it does not run and has thickened to a near-jelly consistency, it's ready for the jars.

Skim any remaining foam from the surface. At this point, you can pour the jam through a mesh strainer to remove as many of the seeds as possible, or just jump right to transferring jam into prepared sterilized jars. Leave 1/4 inch head space, and process in a hot bath for 11 minutes to set. Remove and let cool.

Makes 12 cups.

Nashville is steeped in the tradition of paper. It is home to Hatch Show Print, a letterpress studio in operation since 1879 that is now owned by the Country Music Hall of Fame. It is historically home to paper makers, print makers, and book binders. And it continues that tradition with a vibrant printmaking community that still exists today, as the host of Handmade and Bound, an annual book arts festival that celebrates artists with a connection to paper and print.

This makes Nashville the perfect base of operations for bookmaker Katie Gonzalez. Katie's love affair with hand bound books began in Cortona, Italy, when she took a bookbinding and paper making class while studying abroad during college. When she returned home, she finished her degree in graphic design, but found ways to incorporate book arts into all of her projects, including designing and hand binding a series of three books for her senior thesis project. After graduation, she worked as a graphic designer, but continued bookmaking for herself and friends. She began selling her books on Etsy, gradually moving to part-time outside work, and then making the jump to full-time artist six years ago when she and her husband moved to Nashville. Today, Katie continues to sell her work all over the world through Etsy, and she has started showing her work at a handful of local art shows, including the Porter Flea and Handmade and Bound. In addition, she teaches bookbinding classes at Watkins College of Art, Design & Film, located in Nashville.

As with most functional arts, there are many different methods of bookbinding. Katie walked me through the process she uses by starting with preparing the book's pages. Katie starts with large pieces of paper and then, to get a soft edge on the pages, she folds, creases, and tears each sheet by hand. The pages are then folded in half to create a folded packet of pages, and then holes are punched through the fold where the binding will be sewn.

The book cover is the next step in the process. Katie explains that hard covers for books are made from backboard – a dense, archival cardboard – that can be wrapped with decorative paper or fabric. In fact, Katie recently collaborated with a local weaving company that produced yards of woven fabric, which Katie then cut, backed with paper, and glued onto the backboard to create one-of-a-kind fabric-covered books like those pictured to the left.

Katie also uses handmade paper for her covers, including some that she makes herself. In fact, the namesakes of her business are three textured paper finishes: linen, laid, and felt. To make paper, Katie blends up paper pulp using a beater, which resembles a really heavy-duty blender. The pulp can be comprised of recycled paper, or even recycled cotton or denim fibers. Next, she scoops some of the blended mixture into a big tub of water, and then presses and flattens it onto a very fine screen called a mould and deckle. All of the excess water is squeezed out as the mixture is pressed into the screen, and when it dries, the result is handmade paper.

Katie has also screen printed the paper for her covers, and recently has began experimenting with creating marbled paper. One of her favorite types of book covers, though, is a soft leather, because "the way that leather books are bound means that you can see the stitching on the spine of the book, so you can actually see how it's held together."

Once the paper is created or chosen and prepared, and the cover is created, the next step is to bind the book. When creating leather or woven fabric books, Katie used a four-needle coptic binding. "You are actually sewing with four needles at a time. There are two colors of thread, and then on each of those strands of thread, you have a needle at each end. This allows for a two-color woven binding, and the structure of the binding really comes through because you can see the alternating stitches."

Linen Laid Felt

Artist: Katie Gonzalez

Website: www.linenlaidfelt.com

Instagram: linenlaidfelt

Products: Handbound journals, sketchbooks, photo albums, wedding guest books, and more

Classes: Taught at Watkins College

Katie creates all different sizes and styles of handmade books, but with each book, her mission is the same: to inspire people to actually use their handmade books. She asks customers to send in photos of how they use their books, and to post photos on Instagram, to inspire others to do the same. "Once people do use them, they're so excited," she says. The possibilities are endless: wedding guest books, photo albums for a special trip, baby books, notebooks of daily life, sketchbooks, diaries, garden journals, recipe books, just to name a few. Katie makes a book specially sized to hold square-shaped Instagram photos, for customers who want to create a real-life version of their Instagram feed. She explains that she strives "to make functional art and share ideas for how I've used books, and to collect ideas from other people."

The Nashville community contributes to Katie's work and is part of what makes it possible for her to work full-time as an artist. She notes the role that Nashville's history of book publishing and strong tradition of printmaking plays, and that "there is a strong creative community here, but also a wider community that supports and buys the arts. There is enthusiastic support of the arts scene here in town. I think that having the creative energy of the music scene contributes to the support of the creative community here in Nashville, and the acceptance of nontraditional career paths." ⌘

NATURAL DYE SUPPLY

LOCALLY FORAGED COLOR FROM THE TENNESSEE COUNTRYSIDE

When you arrive at the Fiber Farm, you're first greeted by the farmhouse—originally a two-room log cabin built in the 1860s, it has been added to bit by bit and now welcomes visitors with a wide front porch, complete with rocking chairs. Behind the farmhouse is an old converted garage with space to work with and display the wool and alpaca fleece produced on the farm. Next, you walk across the field to a barn sheltering a small herd of alpacas in a pleasing variety of browns, blacks, and whites; Penelope the sheep and a friendly goat; and a close-knit cluster of three miniature donkeys whose job is it safeguard the other animals. As you walk through the barn toward the back of the acreage, you enter a bit of wilderness: organic paths criss-cross through the trees, you pass a shiitake mushroom log garden. and then come to the land's end, where two smaller streams converge into the Little Fiery Gizzard Creek. You are likely accompanied by Freddie Krueger, the sweet but careworn rescue dog who wandered onto the farm not too long ago and was accepted into the fold, as well as several visiting beagles who have come over from the neighboring farm for a romp through the woods.

Under a black walnut tree in the backyard, you'll find a home-built outdoor fireplace with steeping dye pots, where natural dyes are being created from Osage wood chips, sumac, and the same black walnuts that grow on the branches above you. Nearby is a small area set aside for growing vegetables and dye plants in raised beds framed by recycled bricks.

Every corner of the Fiber Farm provides something new to discover. This is its mission: to provide a place where visitors of all ages can come to see a working farm and learn about the homestead arts. Our host Kacie Lynn offers farm tours, conducts workshops on fiber arts and natural dyes, and sells a selection of handcrafted goods made from the fleece of the farm's res-

ident alpacas. She is excited about collaborating with others who have a skill to teach and are interested in using the space or combining their skills with hers to provide unique learning opportunities. The tagline for Fiber Farm is "*home grown textiles from the Cumberland Plateau*," and Kacie's website describes the site as "a working farm, gathering space, and textile education sanctuary."

On the day we visit, the sun is shining, the alpacas are eager to visit once we have some pellets to hand-feed them, and the dogs excitedly accompany us as we wander through the back woods. It's hard to imagine a more idyllic place, and Kacie is a gracious and knowledge-able host. Originally from Tennessee, she attended college in the south, completing a degree in apparel design and learning about the environ-mental cost of the fashion industry. She lived in Seattle for a while, working in the graphic arts field, before returning home and finding a way to follow her passion for sustainable and ecological fiber arts by acquiring the small farm and then, gradually, its inhabitants.

Kacie gives us a glimpse of all of the fiber projects she has in various stages of production. The farm is truly sheep to needle, as Kacie does everything from raising the animals, to shearing, to scouring and card-ing the wool or alpaca fleece, to spinning and dyeing the yarn. It's a small microcosm of the entire fiber cycle, from start to finish, and a visit to Kacie's farm is a not-to-be-missed experience for any fiber lover. ⌘

Fiber Farm

Host: Kacie Lynn

Location: Tracy City, Tennessee

Phone: 423.280.4004

E-mail: kacie@fiberfarm.net

Website: www.fiberfarm.net

Instagram: fiberfarm

Facebook:
facebook.com/southerntextiles

Offerings:
* Farm tours
* Textile education
* Workshops / retreats
* Photography + design

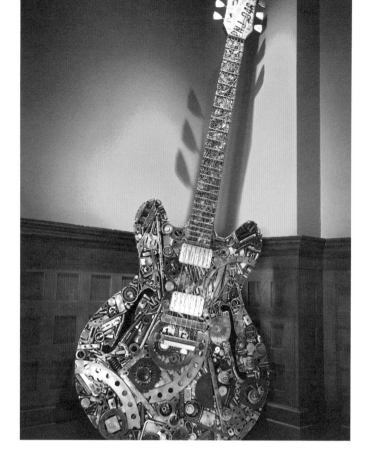

Nashville landmarks include the Parthenon (bottom right), a full-scale replica of the original in Athens, built in 1897 as part of the Tennessee Centennial Exposition for the Bicentennial; and the stately exterior (top left) and baroque interior (bottom left) of Union Station, opened as Nashville's main rail station in 1900, now a luxury hotel.

Local Yarn: Camellia Fiber Company

Camellia Fiber Company founder Rebekka Seele brings a unique combination of artistic talents to the creation of CFC yarns. A hand-spinner since high school, Rebekka has an innate sense for fiber that is pleasing to the eye and the hand. A portion of CFC's monthly shop updates always include handspun yarn, and other CFC yarns are just as intriguing. For instance, CFC Plume is a single-ply merino described as "a marshmallow fluff of a yarn," that brings both loft and halo when knitted up. CFC Flax DK combines alpaca, silk, and flax to create a yarn that has the soft hand of alpaca, the drape and shine of silk, and the strength and structure of flax – perfect for sweaters and shawls.

Rebekka also brings an artist's eye for colors to CFC's yarn dyes. A studio art major in college with a specialty in oil painting, as well as a working illustrator, Rebekka began dyeing with natural dyes—including madder root, wood chips, and marigolds sourced from a friend's backyard garden. CFC now uses environmentally friendly, sustainable dyes. "We dye in tiny batches—10 skeins at a time—which allows us to have a lot of control." Rebekka explains that with her background in color theory and painting, "I can mix only a few primary colors to get a very specific shade of whatever color I am envisioning."

The fiber combinations in CFC yarns, combined with an artist's approach to coloration, help CFC to stand out in an ever more crowded field of indie yarn dyers. Rebekka, who grew up in Alabama, named the company after Alabama's state flower at her mother's suggestion, and ran the business herself for a number of years. However, as the company grew, Rebekka realized that "I have a lot of creative vision, but I'm a terrible business person," and so in November she transferred ownership to Silbia Ro, who had already been assisting her. Rebekka continues to work with CFC's social media, customer service, and creative consult, while Silbia handles production, shipping, and other business-related needs.

Silbia is herself an artist—an illustrator and a calligrapher—and she learned how to knit and spin from Rebekka after the two met at a workshop. The partnership between Silbia and Rebekka epitomizes how two makers are able to make a creative endeavor into a successful business through their combined strengths and skill sets. ⌘

Camellia Fiber Company

Yarnists: Rebekka Seele and Silbia Ro

Website:
www.camelliafibercompany.com

Instagram: camelliafibercompany

Products: Small-batch hand dyed and hand spun yarns

Camellia Cardigan

by Andrea Hungerford

I am always in search of the perfect transitional cardigan, warm enough for early spring days and cool fall evenings, but lightweight enough to wear well over summer dresses. I wanted the neckline and the front band to curve inward, so that it provided sufficient coverage in front and wasn't always slipping off to the sides, and I wanted sleeves that were snug enough that they could be pushed up if the wearer was so inclined. Because I was using Camellia Fiber Company's beautiful Flax DK yarn, I wanted a design that was simple and elegant, to allow the yarn's shine and drape to take center stage.

The Camellia Cardigan looks stunning in any soft summery color; it is designed to be worn with 2-3" of positive ease. The hem length can easily be raised or lowered, depending on personal preference. The pattern is written with garter stitches incorporated into the knitting of the front panels, so that the neckband is knit up at the same time as the fronts—a nice treat at the end, when you realize that the neckband is already complete! However, optionally you can forego the garter stitches at the beginning or end of each front panel row, and instead pick up stitches and knit a garter neckband that runs vertically. This option is modeled in the Camellia Cardigan knit in Pomegranate. Options for the amount of ease, the body length, and the neckband give each knitter easy alternatives to customize the cardigan as they like.

While I know that seaming a sweater together is an extra step, in this case, I chose to design the cardigan in pieces because the seams provide extra structure and stability – an important factor when using yarn that has the qualities of drape and softness that the alpaca and silk bring to CFC Flax DK yarn.

FINISHED MEASUREMENTS

Bust circumference 33 (36, 39, 42.5, 45.5, 48)"
Length from shoulder 25.25 (25.5, 26, 26.25, 26.5, 26.75)"
Shown in size 39"

MATERIALS

Camellia Fiber Company Flax DK (50% alpaca, 25% linen, 25% silk; 270 yds / 247 m per skein)
4 (4, 4, 5, 5, 5) skeins in Silver Sage or Pomegranate

US 5 (3.75 mm) straight needles
Yarn needle, stitch marker

GAUGE

20 sts and 28 rows = 4" in stockinette stitch and garter stripe pattern, blocked

NOTES

Back and fronts are worked in separate pieces from the top down, in a stitch pattern of wide stockinette and narrow garter stripes. Lower edge of body is finished with a turned hem. Sleeves are worked flat from the bottom up in stockinette stitch with a sideways garter stitch cuff.

Pattern includes 1-st selvedges at each seamed edge. These stitches are included in the schematic measurements but not in the finished bust measurement above.

GARTER STRIPE PATTERN

Row 1 (WS): Purl.
Row 2 (RS): Knit.
Rows 3-22: Repeat Rows 1 and 2 ten times.
Rows 23-28: Knit.
Repeat Rows 1-28 for pattern.

PATTERN

BACK

CO 64 (68, 70, 74, 76, 80) sts.
Row 1 (WS): K1 (selvedge st), work in garter stripe pattern to last st, k1 (selvedge st).
Row 2 (RS): K1 (selvedge), work in garter stripe pattern to last st, k1 (selvedge).
Continue as set by last 2 rows until piece measures 6 (5.75, 5.25, 5.25, 5, 5.25)", ending with a WS row.
Armhole inc row (RS): K2, m1R, work to last 2 sts, m1L, k2. 2 sts inc'd.
Repeat armhole inc row on every RS row 4 (6, 9, 10, 11, 11) more times. 74 (82, 90, 96, 100, 104) sts.

Next row (WS): Work to end, use the backward loop method to CO 5 (5, 5, 6, 3, 3) sts on right needle.
Next row (RS): Work to end, CO 5 (5, 5, 6, 3, 3) sts on right needle. 84 (92, 100, 108, 106, 110) sts.

Sizes - (-, -, -, 45.5, 48)" only:
Next 2 rows: Work to end, CO - (-, -, -, 5, 6) sts on right needle. - (-, -, -, 116, 122) sts.

All sizes:
Work even in pattern, maintaining 1-st garter selvedges at each edge, until piece measures 18" from last armhole CO row, ending with a RS row.
Next row (WS, turning ridge for hem): Knit.
Beginning with a knit row (RS), work 7 rows in stockinette stitch.
BO all sts.

LEFT FRONT
CO 18 (19, 20, 21, 22, 23) sts.
Row 1 (WS): K1 (selvedge st), work in garter stripe pattern to last 8 sts, pm, k8 (garter band).
Row 2 (RS): K8 (garter band), sl m, work in garter stripe pattern to last st, k1 (selvedge).
Continue as set by last 2 rows for 3 more rows.

Read ahead! Neck and armhole shaping are worked simultaneously.

Neck inc row (RS): K8, sl m, m1R, work to end. 1 st inc'd.
Repeat neck inc row on every 4th row 14 (14, 15, 15, 16, 16) more times, then on every 2nd row 2 (3, 2, 3, 2, 3) times, for a total of 17 (18, 18, 19, 19, 20) sts inc'd at neck edge.

AT THE SAME TIME, when piece measures 6 (5.75, 5.25, 5.25, 5, 5.25)" ending with a WS row, shape armhole:
Armhole inc row (RS): Work to last 2 sts (including any neck incs), m1L, k2. 1 st inc'd.
Repeat armhole inc row on every RS row 4 (6, 9, 10, 11, 11) more times, for a total of 5 (7, 10, 11, 12, 12) sts inc'd at armhole edge.
Work 1 WS row even.

Next row (RS): Work to end, use the backward loop method to CO 5 (5, 5, 6, 3, 3) sts on right needle.

Sizes - (-, -, -, 45.5, 48)" only:
Next row (WS): Work even.
Next row (RS): Work to end, CO - (-, -, -, 5, 6) sts on right needle.

All sizes:
Continue in pattern, maintaining 1-st garter selvedge at side edge and 8-st garter band at front edge, until all neck increases have been worked. When all armhole and neck shaping is complete, you will have 45 (49, 53, 57, 61, 64) sts.
Work even maintaining selvedge and band until piece measures 18" from last armhole CO row, ending with a RS row.
Next row (WS, turning ridge for hem): Knit.
Beginning with a knit row (RS), work 7 rows in stockinette stitch.
BO all sts.

RIGHT FRONT
CO 18 (19, 20, 21, 22, 23) sts.
Row 1 (WS): K8 (garter band),
pm, work in garter stripe pattern
to last st, k1 (selvedge st).
Row 2 (RS): K1 (selvedge), work
in garter stripe pattern to last 8
sts, sl m, k8 (garter band).
Continue as set by last 2 rows for
3 more rows.

Read ahead! Neck and
armhole shaping are worked
simultaneously.

Neck inc row (RS): Work to last 8
sts, m1L, sl m, k8. 1 st inc'd.
Repeat neck inc row on every 4th
row 14 (14, 15, 15, 16, 16) more
times, then on every 2nd row 2
(3, 2, 3, 2, 3) times, for a total of
17 (18, 18, 19, 19, 20) sts inc'd at
neck edge.

AT THE SAME TIME, when piece measures 6 (5.75, 5.25, 5.25, 5, 5.25)" ending with a WS row, shape armhole:
Armhole inc row (RS): K2, m1R, work to end (including any neck incs). 1 st inc'd.
Repeat armhole inc row on every RS row 4 (6, 9, 10, 11, 11) more times, for a total of 5 (7, 10, 11, 12, 12) sts inc'd at armhole edge.

Next row (WS): Work to end, use the backward loop method to CO 5 (5, 5, 6, 3, 3) sts on right needle.

Sizes - (-, -, -, 45.5, 48)" only:
Next row (RS): Work even.
Next row (WS): Work to end, CO - (-, -, -, 5, 6) sts on right needle.

All sizes:
Continue in pattern, maintaining 1-st garter selvedge at side edge and 8-st garter band at front edge, until all neck increases have been worked. When all armhole and neck shaping is complete, you will have 45 (49, 53, 57, 61, 64) sts.
Work even maintaining selvedge and band until piece measures 18" from last armhole CO row, ending with a RS row.
Next row (WS, turning ridge for hem): Knit.
Beginning with a knit row (RS), work 7 rows in stockinette stitch.
BO all sts.

SLEEVES
Cuff:
CO 20 sts.
Row 1: Sl 1 pwise wyif, knit to end.
Repeat Row 1 until you have a total of 80 (80, 84, 84, 88, 92) rows (or 40 [40, 42, 42, 44, 46] garter ridges). BO.

Sleeve:
Pick up and knit 40 (40, 42, 42, 44, 46) sts along long edge of cuff (1 st per garter ridge).
Row 1 (WS): K1, p to last st, k1.
Row 2 (RS): Knit.
Continue to work in stockinette with 1 garter selvedge st at each end. Work 3 (1, 1, 1, 1, 1) more row(s) even.
Inc row (RS): K2, m1R, k to last 2 sts, m1L, k2. 2 sts inc'd.
Repeat inc row on every 6 (4, 4, 4, 4, 4)th row 7 (2, 2, 8, 11, 14) more times, then on every 8 (6, 6, 6, 6, 6)th row 2 (9, 9, 5, 3, 1) time(s). 60 (64, 66, 70, 74, 78) sts.
Work even until sleeve measures 14'' including cuff, ending with a WS row.

Shape cap:
BO 5 (5, 5, 6, 5, 6) sts at beg of next 2 rows. 50 (54, 56, 58, 64, 66) sts.

Sizes - (-, -. -, 45.5, 48)'' only:
BO 3 sts at beg of next 2 rows. - (-, -, -, 58, 60) sts.

All sizes:
Dec row (RS): K1, ssk, knit to last 3 sts, k2tog, k1. 2 sts dec'd.
Repeat dec row on every 2nd row 6 (7, 8, 9, 7, 7) more times, then every 4th row 2 (2, 2, 2, 4, 4) times, then every 2nd row again 7 (7, 7, 7, 6, 7) times. 18 (20, 20, 20, 22, 22) sts.
Dec row (WS): K1, p2tog, purl to last 3 sts, ssp, k1. 2 sts dec'd.
Repeat RS dec row on next row, then work WS dec row again.
BO rem 12 (14, 14, 14, 16, 16) sts.

FINISHING
Wet block pieces to schematic measurements. Sew shoulder seams, leaving the 8-st garter bands free. Set sleeves into armholes. Sew side and underarm seams. Fold body hem to WS at turning ridge and slip stitch in place.

Back neck edging:
With RS facing, join yarn and pick up and knit 8 sts from right front garter band, then pick up and knit 1 st from back neck edge.
Row 1 (WS): Ssk, k7.
Row 2 (RS): K8, pick up and knit 1 st from back neck edge.
Repeat Rows 1-2 until you have worked all the way across back neck, picking up sts at a rate of 1 st in each CO st. End with a WS row.
Graft (Kitchener stitch) the 8 sts on the needle to the CO end of the left neck band. Alternatively, you may BO the stitches on the needle and seam neatly to the CO end of the left neck band.

Weave in ends. Steam the seams and back neck edging.

ABBREVIATIONS

BO   bind off/bound-off

CO   cast on/cast-on

dec('d) decrease(d)

inc('d) increase(d)

K   knit

K2tog   knit two stitches together

M   marker

MIL   make 1 left: with right needle, pick up running thread between needles from back to front and place it on left needle, then knit it through the back loop

MIR   make 1 right: with right needle, pick up running thread between needles from front to back, place on left needle, knit it through the front loop

P   purl

Pm   place marker

P2tog   purl 2 together

Pwise   purlwise/as if to purl

Rem   remain

Rep   repeat

RLI   right lifted increase: knit into right side of stitch 1 row below next st on left needle

Rnd(s) round(s)

RS   right side

Sl   slip

St(s)   stitch(es)

Ssk   [slip 1 as if to knit] 2 times, insert left needle into fronts of these sts and knit them together

Ssp   [slip 1 as if to knit] 2 times, transfer these sts back to the left needle (st mount is reversed), p2tog through the back loop

WS   wrong side

Wyif   with yarn in front

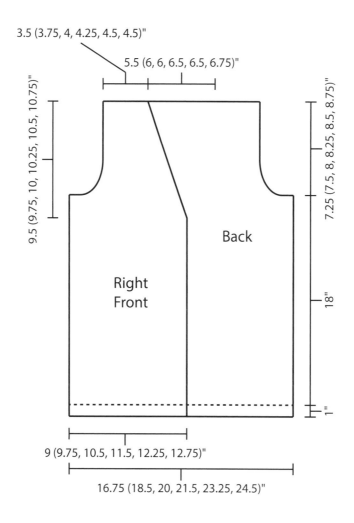

3.5 (3.75, 4, 4.25, 4.5, 4.5)"

5.5 (6, 6, 6.5, 6.5, 6.75)"

9.5 (9.75, 10, 10.25, 10.5, 10.75)"

7.25 (7.5, 8, 8.25, 8.5, 8.75)"

Back

Right Front

18"

1"

9 (9.75, 10.5, 11.5, 12.25, 12.75)"

16.75 (18.5, 20, 21.5, 23.25, 24.5)"

Creating Community: Mason-Dixon Knitting

Mason-Dixon Knitting is about using a common interest—in this case, knitting—to form a virtual community. "Knitting's not really about knitting," explains Ann Shayne, the southern "Dixon" half of the Mason-Dixon team. "Different people use it in different ways, but for me, it has to do with community…I started knitting when I had little kids and I had small chunks of time throughout the day to pick up the needles. What I didn't have was time to go to the yarn store and hang out with other knitters. The Internet had just emerged as a place where you could meet people who were just as crazy about knitting as you were. The community part is sharing a fascination of something with people who are as curious about it as you are."

MDK got its start as a relationship between penpals. Ann Shayne, who had moved back to her home town of Nashville to raise her family, met Kay Gardiner, who was living in New York and also raising small children, on an Internet message board. The two began a discussion about the same Rowan sweater pattern that they both were knitting. "After a few months, we realized we were writing a lot. We both had little kids, were both kind of type A, and had both quit our jobs to stay home with our kids—and I said we should start a blog," Ann recalls.

There were almost no knitting blogs at that time, and the start of the blog led to a discussion about book ideas. "We wanted to do something fun and different than what we'd seen—a how-to book with beautiful pictures, and patterns that were easy but had some interesting features," says Ann. It wasn't until a deal had been struck for the Mason-Dixon Knitting book that Ann and Kay actually met in person.

The online presence of MDK has evolved, and now its recently reformulated site provides an entire virtual world of ways for knitters to connect. Ann and Kay work to post something new on the site every single day, and have incorporated the work of other writers and guest contributors. Ann notes that "our contributors are people we admire. We want their work on our site, and we think our readers will enjoy what they have to say." Recent contributions include Knitstrips (comic strips that are also knitting patterns); a Slow Cooker Odyssey of recipes; A Knitter's Weekend series that shares good knitting spots around the country through photo essays; and a series on color theory by designer and writer Ann Weaver.

The content of MDK changes every day and is categorized as:

* Letters – "A correspondence that started in 2003. Enter if you dare."
* How To – "Tips, tricks, hints and hacks for the knitter in search of a better way."
* Projects – "The designs we are knitting and admiring."
* Inspiration – "You never know what's going to catch our eye. A compendium of wonders."
* Fun – "A slippery slope of our favorite diversions and distractions."
* Travel – "Adventures near and far, often involving knitting but always in beautiful places."

* Contributors – "Our ever-growing roster of the sparkliest designers and writers."

An online shop was incorporated into the website, as well. "After a while, it just started to seem logical. If you're going to tell knitters about products you love, wouldn't you want them to be able to buy those things?" Ann explains that they didn't want to write another big pattern book, but instead have started writing a series of "field guides"—small pamphlets that explore a single knitting concept or component through narrative and patterns. The online store then stocks kits based on the field guides, which allows Ann and Kay to share yarns they particularly love with their readers.

Another feature of MDK is the just-launched Year of Techniques. "A friend of ours in England who is a tech editor is launching a new technique every month, and then creating an e-mail and a tech book, and MDK is promoting the whole program. This is going to be a big teaching piece for us," explains Ann. The MDK site will host a monthly techniques video, which will be tied to a different pattern for each technique. This will give knitters a chance to explore new challenges by knitting a series of patterns specifically designed to help them expand their technical skills.

MDK also includes its own message board—"a virtual community site," as Ann describes it—and plans are in the works for an MDK retreat in 2018 at Shakerag, an arts retreat center located in Sewanee, Tennessee. "It's hard to track down people who are as obsessed as you are about knitting in real life. That's the reason for the message board and the creation of virtual community, and why we decided to host our first retreat. The community is virtual, but you still want to meet the people!" ⌘

Mason-Dixon Knitting

Creators: Ann Shayne and Kay Gardiner

Website: www.masondixonknitting.com

Instagram: mason.dixon.knitting

Ravelry: ravelry.com/patterns/sources/mason-dixon-knitting

Content: Message board, online shop, knitting projects and designs, tips and techniques, inspiration and fun, travel and events for knitters, articles written by over two dozen contributors

Publications: Mason-Dixon Knitting; A Coloring Book for Knitters; and Field Guides No. 1 (Stripes), No. 2 (Fair Isle), and No. 3 (Wild Yarns)

Spring Planting: Succulents

Succulents offer an infinite variety of leaf shapes, sizes, colors, and textures. They are quick to pot up, easy to grow, and bring a pop of nature into any room. Part of the fun is all of the different materials you can use to house them: wooden boxes, stone urns, galvanized metal pots, or glass jars, to name a few. As pictured above, I used log rounds in a variety of heights, salvaged from our downed cherry tree, to create a multi-level "stage" on the island in our kitchen for my collection of succulents.

Crackerjack Jersey Top

by Andrea Hungerford

A fresh take on the classic baseball jersey, this top is the perfect spring staple for your wardrobe. Choose your favorite bright color to contrast with a crisp white, or use a solid color for the body and a complementary gradient for the sleeves. Wear the sleeves cuffed or uncuffed, or knit them longer for a three-quarter length.

Note: The raglan seams are joined by picking up stitches along each edge then binding them off together with a three-needle bind off, to create the look of an exposed seam that nicely joins the differing colors of the body and the sleeve. You have the option of skipping this step and simply mattress seaming these edges instead.

FINISHED MEASUREMENTS
Bust circumference 33 (35, 37, 39) (41, 43, 45, 47)"
Length from shoulder to lowest point of hem 25.25 (25.5, 25.75, 26) (26.75, 27.25, 27.5, 27.75)"

Shown in size 39"

MATERIALS
Camellia Fiber Company Merino Sport (100% merino wool, 325 yds / 297 m per 100 g skein)
2 (2, 2, 2) (3, 3, 3, 3) skeins in Ivory (MC)
1 (1, 1, 1) (2, 2, 2, 2) skeins in Clementine (CC)

US 4 (3.5 mm) straight needles
US 3 (3.25 mm) 16" circular needle
Yarn needle, stitch marker

GAUGE
24 sts and 32 rows = 4" in stockinette st on larger needles, blocked

NOTES
Top is knit flat in pieces, all worked from the neck down to the hem. Short rows shape the curved lower edge on back and front. Raglan seams are joined with picked-up stitches and three-needle bind offs; side and underarm seams are sewn using mattress stitch. Collar is picked up around neck edge and worked in the round.

Pattern includes 1-st selvedges at each seamed edge. These stitches are included in the schematic measurements but not in the finished bust measurement above.

PATTERN
BACK
With larger needles and MC, CO 45 (45, 47, 47) (49, 49, 51, 51) sts. Knit 1 row. Purl 1 row.

Shape raglan:
Inc row (RS): K2, RLI, knit to last 2 sts, LLI, k2. 2 sts inc'd.
Continue in stockinette, rep inc row on every 2nd row 13 (13, 13, 13) (29, 30, 31, 32) more times, then on every 4th row 4 (3, 2, 1) (-, -, -, -) time(s), then on every 2nd row again 4 (7, 10, 13) (-, -, -, -) times. 89 (93, 99, 103) (109, 111, 115, 117) sts.
Work 1 WS row even.
Next row (RS): Knit to end, use the backward loop method to CO 6 (7, 7, 8) (8, 3, 3, 5) sts.
Next row (WS): Purl to end, use the backward loop method to CO 6 (7, 7, 8) (8, 3, 3, 5) sts. 101 (107, 113, 119) (125, 117, 121, 127) sts.

Sizes - (-, -, -) (-, 43, 45, 47)" only:
Next row (RS): Knit to end, use the backward loop method to CO - (-, -, -) (-, 7, 8, 8) sts.
Next row (WS): Purl to end, use the backward loop method to CO - (-, -, -) (-, 7, 8, 8) sts. - (-, -, -) (-, 131, 137, 143) sts.
Lower body (all sizes):
Work even until piece measures 14 (14, 14, 14) (14.5, 14.5, 14.5, 14.5)" from last underarm CO, ending with a WS row.

Shape curved hem:
Short row 1 (RS): Knit to last 2 (2, 3, 3) (3, 3, 3, 3) sts, turn.

Short row 2 (WS): GSR, purl to last 2 (2, 3, 3) (3, 3, 3, 3) sts, turn.

Short row 3: GSR, work to 3 (4, 4, 4) (4, 4, 5, 5) sts before previous turning point, turn.

Repeat last row 1 (13, 11, 7) (5, 3, 13, 13) more time(s).

Next short row: GSR, work to 4 (5, 5, 5) (5, 5, 5, 6) sts before previous turning point, turn.

Repeat last row 13 (1, 3, 7) (9, 11, 1, 1) more time(s).

Next row (RS): GSR, knit to end, knitting through both legs of each "double" stitch.

Next row (WS): Purl to end, purling through both legs of each "double" stitch.

Sizes 33 (-, 37, -) (41, -, 45, -)" only:
Rib set-up row (RS): *K2, p2; rep from * to last st, LLI, k1. 102 (-, 114, -) (126, -, 138, -) sts.

Sizes – (35, -, 39) (-, 43, -, 47)" only:
Rib set-up row (RS): *K2, p2; rep from * to last 3 sts, k2tog, k1. - (106, -, 118) (-, 130, -, 142) sts.

All sizes:
Rib row 1 (WS): *P2, k2; rep from * to last 2 sts, p2.
Rib row 2 (RS): *K2, p2; rep from * to last 2 sts, k2.
Rep these 2 rows once more, then rib row 1 again.
BO all sts in rib.

FRONT
Left side neck and raglan:
With larger needles and MC, CO 4 sts. Knit 1 row. Purl 1 row.
Raglan inc row (RS): Knit to last 2 sts, LLI, k2. 1 st inc'd at raglan edge.
Purl 1 row.
Rep the last 2 rows 1 (1, 1, 1) (2, 2, 2, 2) more time(s). 6 (6, 6, 6) (7, 7, 7, 7) sts.
Neck and raglan inc row (RS): K2, RLI, knit to last 2 sts, LLI, k2. 1 st inc'd at raglan edge and 1 st inc'd at neck edge.
Continue in stockinette, rep neck and raglan inc row on every 2nd row 9 more times. 26 (26, 26, 26) (27, 27, 27, 27) sts.

Work 1 WS row even.
Cut yarn and place sts on holder.

Right side neck and raglan:
With larger needles and MC, CO 4 sts. Knit 1 row. Purl 1 row.
Raglan inc row (RS): K2, RLI, knit to end. 1 st inc'd at raglan edge.
Purl 1 row.
Rep the last 2 rows 1 (1, 1, 1) (2, 2, 2, 2) more time(s). 6 (6, 6, 6) (7, 7, 7, 7) sts.
Neck and raglan inc row (RS): K2, RLI, knit to last 2 sts, LLI, k2. 1 st inc'd at raglan edge and 1 st inc'd at neck edge.
Continue in stockinette, rep neck and raglan inc row on every 2nd row 9 more times. 26 (26, 26, 26) (27, 27, 27, 27) sts. Work 1 WS row even. Leave sts on needle.

Join fronts and cast on for center front neck (RS): K2, RLI, knit to end of right front, use the backward loop method to CO 17 (17, 19, 19, 21, 21, 23, 23) sts, place left front sts on left needle with RS facing, then knit across to last 2 sts, LLI, k2. 71 (71, 73, 73) (77, 77, 79, 79) sts.

Complete raglan shaping:
Work 1 WS row even.
Inc row: K2, RLI, knit to last 2 sts, LLI, k2. 2 sts inc'd.
Rep inc row on every 2nd row - (-, -, -) (15, 16, 17, 18) more times, then on every 4th row 4 (3, 2, 1) (-, -, -, -) time(s), then on every 2nd row again 4 (7, 10, 13) (-, -, -, -) times. 89 (93, 99, 103) (109, 111, 115, 117) sts. Work 1 WS row even.
Next row (RS): Knit to end, use the backward loop method to CO 6 (7, 7, 8) (8, 3, 3, 5) sts.
Next row (WS): Purl to end, use the backward loop method to CO 6 (7, 7, 8) (8, 3, 3, 5) sts. 101 (107, 113, 119) (125, 117, 121, 127) sts.

Sizes - (-, -, -) (-, 43, 45, 47)" only:
Next row (RS): Knit to end, use the backward loop method to CO - (-, -, -) (-, 7, 8, 8) sts.
Next row (WS): Purl to end, use the backward loop method to CO - (-, -, -) (-, 7, 8, 8) sts. - (-, -, -) (-, 131,

137, 143) sts.
Lower body (all sizes): Work same as back.

SLEEVES
With larger needles and CC, CO 17 sts. Knit 1 row. Purl 1 row.

Shape raglan:
Inc row: K2, RLI, knit to last 2 sts, LLI, k2. 2 sts inc'd.
Continuing in stockinette, rep inc row on every 2nd row 7 (8, 9, 10) (11, 11, 11, 11) more times, then on every 4th row 5 (5, 4, 4) (3, 4, 4, 5) times, then on every 2nd row again 8 (8, 10, 10) (12, 11, 12, 11) times. 59 (61, 65, 67) (71, 71, 73, 73) sts.
Work 1 WS row even.
Next row (RS): Knit to end, use the backward loop method to CO 6 (7, 7, 8) (8, 3, 3, 5) sts.
Next row (WS): Purl to end, use the backward loop method to CO 6 (7, 7, 8) (8, 3, 3, 5) sts. 71 (75, 79, 83) (87, 77, 79, 83) sts.
Sizes - (-, -, -) (-, 43, 45, 47)" only:
Next row (RS): Knit to end, use the backward loop method to CO - (-, -, -) (-, 7, 8, 8) sts.
Next row (WS): Purl to end, use the backward loop method to CO - (-, -, -) (-, 7, 8, 8) sts. - (-, -, -) (-, 91, 95, 99) sts.

Shape underarm (all sizes):
Work 8 rows even, ending with a WS row.
Dec row (RS): K1, ssk, knit to last 3 sts, k2tog, k1. 2 sts dec'd.
Rep dec row on every 10th row 3 more times. 63 (67, 71, 75) (79, 83, 87, 91) sts remain.
Work even until sleeve measures 5.5" from last underarm CO or desired length, ending with a RS row.
Next row (WS, turning ridge for hem): Knit.
Beginning with a knit row (RS), work 7 rows in stockinette. BO.

FINISHING
Block pieces to schematic measurements.

Using larger needles and CC, with RS facing pick up and knit 3 sts for every 4 rows and 1 st in every CO st along front right raglan edge, then with another strand of CC pick up and knit the same number of stitches along corresponding sleeve edge. Holding the pieces with wrong sides together, join the two sets of stitches with a three-needle bind off in CC. Keep the bind off loose so as not to cause puckering in the seam. Repeat for the other three raglan seams.

Using smaller circular needles and CC, with RS facing and beginning at back left raglan seam, pick up and knit 1 st in each CO st and 2 sts in every 3 rows all around neckline. Adjust as necessary to achieve a multiple of 4 sts. Place marker for beg of round.
Rib rnd: *K2, p2; rep from * to end.
Rep rib rnd 5 more times. BO in rib.
Sew side and sleeve seams. Weave in ends. Block again if desired.

ABBREVIATIONS

BO   bind off/bound-off

dec('d) decrease(d)

GSR   German short row (see Techniques)

K   knit

LLI   left lifted increase: knit into left side of stitch 2 rows below last st on right needle

P   purl

Rep   repeat

RLI   right lifted increase: knit into right side of stitch 1 row below next st on left needle

RS   right side

Ssk   [slip 1 as if to knit] 2 times, insert left needle into fronts of these sts and knit them together

St(s)   stitch(es)

CO   cast on/cast-off

inc('d) increase(d)

K2tog   knit two stitches together

Pm   place marker

Rnd(s) round(s)

Sl   slip

WS   wrong side

TECHNIQUES

German Short Rows

GSR: Slip 1 purlwise with yarn in front, then pull yarn up and over needle to back, drawing the two "legs" of the slipped stitch up. This creates what looks like a double stitch. When you work back over the "double" stitch later, knit or purl it through both legs.

Three-Needle Bind Off

Have the two pieces to be joined on separate needles held together in the left hand. Using a third needle, insert into first st on front needle, then first st on back needle and knit them together. *Insert into next st on front needle, then next st on back needle and knit them together, then pass first st on right needle over second to BO 1 st. Repeat from *.

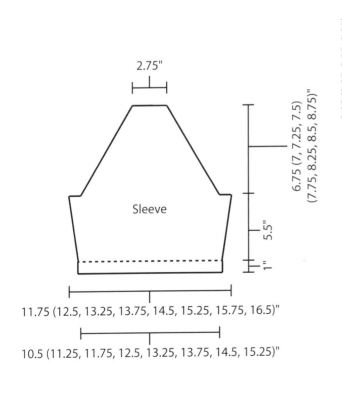

2.75"

Sleeve

6.75 (7, 7.25, 7.5) (7.75, 8.25, 8.5, 8.75)"

5.5"

1"

11.75 (12.5, 13.25, 13.75, 14.5, 15.25, 15.75, 16.5)"

10.5 (11.25, 11.75, 12.5, 13.25, 13.75, 14.5, 15.25)"

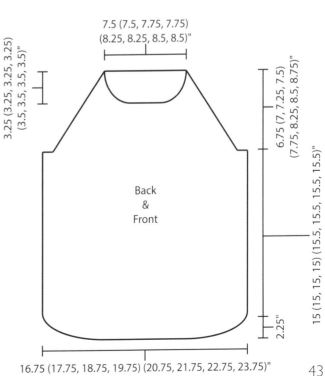

7.5 (7.5, 7.75, 7.75)
(8.25, 8.25, 8.5, 8.5)"

3.25 (3.25, 3.25, 3.25)
(3.5, 3.5, 3.5, 3.5)"

Back
&
Front

6.75 (7, 7.25, 7.5)
(7.75, 8.25, 8.5, 8.75)"

15 (15, 15, 15) (15.5, 15.5, 15.5, 15.5)"

2.25"

16.75 (17.75, 18.75, 19.75) (20.75, 21.75, 22.75, 23.75)"

The party never stops in down-town Nashville, where musicians play seven nights a week in bars up and down Printer's Alley. With the doors propped open, you can stroll down Broadway and listen to the music as it rolls out into the night air.

44

Handcrafted Leather: Hunker Bag Co.

Hunker Bag Co.'s origins are rooted in creator Denton Hunker's musical career as a drummer for the band Green River Ordinance. Denton has known how to sew since high school, when his grandmother taught him the basics so that he could sew his own clothes. "When the band started touring a lot," he explains, "we were flying and I had this little black roller suitcase. Twice someone else took it at the baggage claim because it looked like every other bag. So I decided to make myself a bag. I went and got some leather and canvas and made the duffel bag that is now the model I sell through Hunker Bag Co. I used it for a really long time while we were touring and people would always ask me where I bought it."

Denton was sewing for another company that made high-end women's bags during his time off the road, and so when the band started slowing down, "I wanted to have my own creative outlet"—and Hunker Bag Co. was born. Starting about two years ago, Denton purchased an industrial sewing machine and began making the bags as what he describes as "a DIY kind of thing." Later, he bought additional machines for his one-man shop to upgrade the designs and create the bags more efficiently.

The workshop for Hunker Bag Co. is a garage that Denton spent an entire month renovating himself. His sewing techniques are largely self-taught, gained through trial and error.

Denton notes that going from a hobby to a production level of creating is exciting, and brings its own set of challenges. "There's never enough time in the day to cover everything, including the aspect of running a business. My hope is that I can turn what I love to do into something that is sustainable over time."

Tapping into the fan base that already existed for Green River Ordinance gave him an immediate client base, and since its inception, most all of Hunker Bag Co.'s bags are sold online. The bags are crafted from waxed canvas and leather, with brass hardware; Denton notes that "I love the textures and colors of the waxed canvas, and the durability of the leather." He sews each one of the bags completely by hand, using the variety of sewing machines in his shop. The colors are earth tones—grays, greens, and blues. "I feel that my bags have this outdoor kind of vibe—classy but rugged."

Denton creates a wide variety of styles for both men and women, from the original duffel bag to messenger, trail, and toiletry bags; wallets, clutches, and both small and large cross-body bags; and totes and backpacks. Some of the larger bags, like the duffels, have rope handles, created with a technique called whipping that Denton learned in Boy Scouts. It's a technique of putting cord on the ends of the ropes to keep them from fraying, and it is very time-consuming and laborious, taking about 1 ½ to 2 hours to attach the rope to a single bag.

Nashville has been a welcome home for Denton's creative inclinations. "It's just easier to do anything here creatively, there are so many creative people around, and they're all so eager to help you out. There's no sense of competition even if other artists are doing the same kind of work. It's been such a welcome community. You get here and you immediately feel more creative." ⌘

Hunker Bag Co.

Creator: Denton Hunker

Website: www.hunkerbagco.com

Instagram: hunkerbagco

Products: duffel, trail, rolltop, mail pouch, messenger, tote, backpack, clutch, wallet, toiletry, small and cross-body, brief, pouch

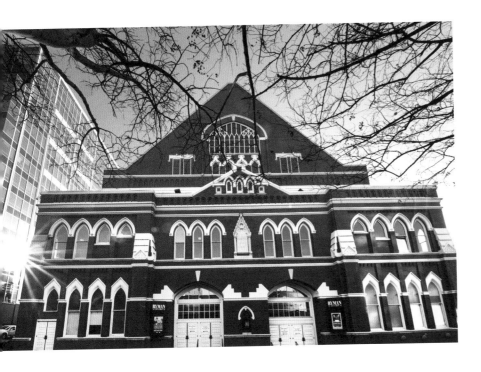

Ryman Auditorium, known as the "church of country music," opened as the Union Gospel Tabernacle in 1892, and housed the Grand Ole Opry from 1943 to 1974.

Colorful stained glass windows adorn the north-facing side of the Ryman.

Local Yarn Store: Haus of Yarn

Haus of Yarn has space—lots of it. Many yarns stores are crammed into tiny, quaint settings with narrow rooms and yarns stacked to the ceiling, and we love them for it. But Haus of Yarn gives shoppers a different experience. It is open and welcoming, with room to breathe and wander in a light-filled setting. The yarns are displayed thoughtfully and beautifully, in ways that let you see their individual colors and textures, and very often with a sample knit that inspires you to go beyond just fondling the yarn to actually planning how to knit it up for your next project.

Store manager Meg Strong takes advantage of this spacious setting by stocking the store full of the best variety of yarns imaginable to meet a knitter at any level of skill or interest. Although Meg is a self-professed lover of grays—"all the grays, it's my jam; I love how my stitches look in gray"—she has an eye for color and an instinct for how to arrange and display a wide run of colors to draw her customers in. All of the basics are amply covered. There are complete runs of color in the reasonably priced Encore, and a huge selection of Malbrigo. But Meg has also carefully curated a wonderful selection of top-notch brands from all over the world: Brooklyn Tweed, Wollmeise, Cestari, Heirloom Worsted, and Geilsk, just to name a few. She stocks sought-after and hard-to-find indie dyers like Spincycle Yarns and Jill Draper Makes Things, and she recently hosted a trunk show for Plucky Yarns, resulting in a large collection of leftover Plucky colors and bases, some of which aren't available anywhere else. Meg explains that she works to represent all different price points in the yarns she stocks: "We're in a big city, we have a customer base that is very diverse, and we work not to exclude anyone."

Meg also stocks local yarns and products whenever she can. For instance, Haus of Yarn carries Silver Creek Heart Ranch, spun from local alpaca fleeces, and will soon stock Nutmeg Yarns' Icelandic/Targhee yarn, made with 100% Tennessee-sourced wool and spun in North Carolina. Meg explains that the store has a very large out-of-town client base, and so she tries to stock products that are Tennessee-made whenever possible. The store carries Nashville-based Fringe Association's products, locally made project bags, and even beautiful wooden vertical squirrel swifts, handmade by Meg's father. Haus of Yarn also has its own pattern line, created by Meg's mother, inspired by the shape and design of Nashville landmarks such as the Ryman, the Parthenon, and something currently in the works inspired by Union Station.

Haus of Yarn has been in business in the same location for 14 years now, and has created community, as well as a beautiful and well-stocked source for all things fiber-related. Since its opening, classes on beginning knitting and pick-your-project have been held weekly, and more classes are added to the roster all the time. These are taught by part-time instructors who teach specific skills like sock knitting, how to fix your mistakes, and hand looming. The store sponsors trunk shows for indie dyers and yarn designers, and it hosts a year-long knit-along, during which participants knit a different project each month that features a specific skill or technique, to both inspire knitters to complete their projects, and build their knowledge base.

Meg herself is a wonderful ambassador for the store: warm and friendly, with southern charm and a large body of knowledge about yarn, knitting, and what makers who work with fiber need, she makes shopping

at Haus of Yarn a wonderful experience. And if you're in the store on a Friday, you may have the chance to say hi to Stanley, the sweetest rescue pup you'll ever meet. "People come to knitting for all sorts of reasons, but often it's self-care, so I want to help steer our customers toward something that they will be successful and happy with." ⌘

Haus of Yarn

Address: 265 White Bridge Rd., Nashville

Phone: 615.354.1007

E-mail: admin@hausofyarn.com

Website: www.hausofyarn.com

Yarn lines include: Brooklyn Tweed, Wollmeise, Spincycle, Nutmeg Yarns, Heirloom Worsted, Jill Draper Makes Things, Silver Creek Heart Ranch, Geilsk, Cestari

Spring puts on a show at the Cheekwood Botanical Gardens. The gardens, which span 55 acres, also include an art museum housed in a historical estate built in the late 1920s.

Sasanqua Wrap

by Andrea Hungerford

Camellia Fiber Company's Plume is labeled a puffy, light, and luxurious marshmallow-fluff-of-a-yarn, and the description is apt. The single ply construction and the fiber composition of alpaca, merino, and silk create a lighter-than-air hand with the halo of alpaca, the sheen of silk, and the structure of merino. It is a winning combination, and perfect for a lightweight summer wrap.

My inspiration for the Sasanqua Wrap (named for a variety of flowering camellia) was a dainty wrap made to slip around your shoulders when wearing a tank top or strappy summer dress. I didn't want it too long or too wide – a big piece of fabric becomes more of a hindrance than a help, and I'm always struggling to figure out how to wrap it around me or tie it so that it doesn't slip off my shoulders. To address this issue, I borrowed the sewing concept of a gathering stitch—just a simple strand of yarn that allows you to gather the top edge of the wrap as much or as little as you'd like. Pulling the gathers in a bit tightens the top edge of the wrap and allows it to sit more snugly on your shoulders.

FINISHED MEASUREMENTS
Width along top edge (ungathered) 54"
Width along bottom edge 36"
Height 13"

MATERIALS
Camellia Fiber Company Plume (40% alpaca, 40% merino wool,
20% silk; 250 yds / 228 m per 100 g skein)
2 skeins in Ivory (MC)

Shibui Knits Lunar (60% extra fine merino wool, 40% mulberry
silk; 401 yds / 367 m per 50 g skein)
1 skein in Imperial (CC) (see Notes)

US 8 (5 mm) 24" or longer circular needle
US 5 (3.75 mm) 24" or longer circular needle
Yarn needle

GAUGE
22 sts and 19 rows = 4" in lace pattern on larger needle, heavily
blocked

NOTES
Main panel of wrap is knit flat in a long strip, then stitches are picked up along one long edge and a scalloped border is worked. The border draws in the edge somewhat and the final, ungathered shape is approximately trapezoidal.

CC yarn is used triple-stranded, and does not require a full skein; 50 yards should be more than enough. Substitute with another lace weight yarn held triple, or a fingering weight held double.

Slip the first stitch of every row purlwise with yarn in front throughout.

PATTERN
With larger needle and MC, CO 53 sts.
Rows 1 and 2: Sl 1 (see Notes), knit to end.
Row 3 (RS): Sl 1, k3, *k1, yo, k2, skp, k2tog, k2, yo; rep from * to last 4 sts, k4.
Row 4 (WS): Sl 1, k2, purl to last 3 sts, k3.
Row 5: Sl 1, k3, *yo, k2, skp, k2tog, k2, yo, k1; rep from * to last 4 sts, k4.
Row 6: Sl 1, k2, purl to last 3 sts, k3.
Repeat Rows 3-6 sixty-one more times, then work Rows 3 and 4 again.
Next 2 rows: Sl 1, knit to end.
BO all sts.

With smaller needle and three strands of CC held together, RS facing, pick up and knit 127 sts (1 st in every slipped st) along right edge of piece.

Next 3 rows: Sl 1, knit to end.

Change to larger needle and MC.
Row 1 (RS): Sl 1, knit to end.
Row 2: Sl 1, purl to end.
Repeat Rows 1-2 two more times.

Work scalloped edging:
Row 1 (RS): Sl 1 pwise wyif, *[ssk] 3 times, [yo, k1] 5 times, yo, [k2tog] 3 times, k1; repeat from * to end.
Row 2 (WS): Sl 1, purl to end.
Row 3: Sl 1, knit to end.
Row 4: Sl 1, purl to end.
Row 5: Repeat Row 1.
Row 6: Sl 1, purl to end.
Row 7: Sl 1, knit to end.
Row 8: Sl 1, purl to end.
Row 9: Repeat Row 1.
BO all sts knitwise on WS.

FINISHING
Weave in ends but do not trim. Wet-block aggressively to open up lace. When dry, trim ends.

Optional: Using a yarn needle, weave one strand of MC through the top edge of the wrap. Cinch up the top of the wrap into gathers, as much or as little as you want, and evenly distribute the gathers throughout. Weave in the ends of the gathering strand.

ABBREVIATIONS
BO   bind off/bound-off
CC   contrast color
CO   cast on/cast-on
K   knit
K2tog   knit 2 sts together
MC   main color
P   purl
RS   right side
Sl   slip
St(s)   stitch(es)
Skp   slip 1 as if to knit, k1, pass slipped st over the knit st
Ssk   [slip 1 as if to knit] 2 times, insert left needle into fronts of these sts and knit them together
WS   wrong side
Yo   yarn over

Birds of Nashville: the Northern Mockingbird, which is the Tennessee State Bird (top), the Eastern Bluebird (middle), and a male Northern Cardinal (bottom)

Bespoke Cowboy Boots: Music City Leather

In this day and age, it seems like almost anything and everything can be ordered on the Internet. But if you want a pair of cowboy boots custom made for you by Music City Leather, your first step is a face-to-face fitting session with bootmaker Wes Shugart. Your boots will truly be one of a kind, made by hand to fit only you. Wes will take a pedigraph, a tracing, and no less than eight measurements of your foot to start this process—all of which can only be accomplished in person. According to Wes, there are over 360 steps involved in making a cowboy boot by hand, and exacting measurements make up the crucial beginnings of these steps.

Next, you get to select the color and origin of the leather you'd like to use from options that include water buffalo, ostrich, kangaroo, pig, calf, and bison. You also select a stitch design. Bootmakers don't copy another maker's stitch design; so as long as a maker is alive, the accepted custom and practice is that the stitch designs are exclusive to that maker. "There are no original stitch designs," Wes explains. "They've all been passed down from prior generations of bootmakers, like carrying on a lineage." In that way, the history of bootmaking design is literally stitched into the patterns on the boots themselves.

According to Wes, cowboy boots and blue jeans are the only true American-designed fashion, and both arose out of necessity. Blue jeans were first made by gold miners, while the history of cowboy boots began with the Wellington boots worn by soldiers in the Civil War, combined with the influence of the Texas Vaqueros' high-heeled lace-up boots. "By the time they got to Kansas to work on the railroads, the boots had worn out. Cowboy boots were invented in Kansas because the cobblers who repaired boots combined the Vaqueros' style with a taller shaft to protect the leg." Wes explains that the original purpose of the stitching on cowboy boots was to reinforce the boot; the wrinkle at the top of the toe was put in place to protect the boots from chafing against the stirrups; the bug was supposed to give the illusion of a shorter foot; and the high heel and wide leather sole were designed to hold a rider in the stirrups. "Everything on the cowboy boot was originally designed for function. It wasn't until the early

20th century, under the influence of movie stars like Gene Autry and Roy Rogers, that the 'flora and fauna' was added to boots to create more style." By the 60s, the style had died out, and cowboy boots were being worn only in the American west, but the 1970s move "Urban Cowboy" revitalized the boot as a fashion trend.

Wes, who grew up on a Georgia cattle farm, began making cowboy boots as a hobby, but then elevated his knowledge and skill by apprenticing with accomplished bootmakers in Albuquerque and Prescott, Arizona. He completes every step of his custom bootmaking by hand in his home-based shop. Just a few of his customized steps include creating an individualized plastic last for each customer; ghost stitching; hand skiving the leather for a superior fit where two pieces of leather join together; and using leather soles, a penny nail for arch support, and wood posts instead of nails in the sole so that they won't rust. Lead time for Wes to create your custom boots is six to twelve months, and in the past year he has completed 42 pairs.

Even after years of custom bootmaking, Wes still loves the work. "I'm creating functional art, hanging out with my dog, and my commute is 13 feet. Each pair is different, every design is different, because every foot is different. When you hand make you strive for perfection, but you're human, so you'll never achieve it. Where perfection and imperfection meet is where you have real beauty." ⌘

Music City Leather

Bootmaker: Wes Shugart

Website: www.musiccityleather.com

Instagram: musiccityleather

Phone: 615.533.4882

59

"THE BEST WAY
TO PREDICT
THE FUTURE IS
TO DESIGN IT."

BUCKMINSTER FULLER

Where to Learn: Reunion Yarn

Although little Ruby Jean is only a few weeks old, new mom Emily Felix meets me at the door with a smile, looking fresh and beautiful, wearing her baby daughter in a sling. Emily is the creator of Reunion Yarn, and she brings a great deal of education, training, and global ethos to a concept as deceptively simple as unraveling sweaters. After earning a BFA in college, Emily was admitted to the fiber and textiles department of Savannah College of Art and Design (SCAD). There, she discovered an entire curriculum that explored the concepts of sustainability and slow fashion. She describes her first design for sustainability class as a "brain explosion moment... I thought that I had been using yarn that was supposedly eco-friendly, but I realized that when you look into where yarn is really from, and everything that goes into producing it, it's impossible to tell what the ultimate environmental impact really is." Emily went on to embrace the concept of textiles recycling as her thesis while at SCAD, with a focus on using sustainable fibers.

As a "poor college student" looking for sustainable yarn, Emily was inspired by a tutorial she found on Pinterest about how to unravel sweaters. "This process was more fulfilling for me than using the yarn to actually make stuff." Emily explains that the tutorial was poorly made, and she had to learn most of the process on her own through trial and error. "I started refining the process, and my husband [who has taught industrial design at SCAD] helped me build machines to speed up the process." All of this led to the launch of Reunion Yarn in 2015.

The process of creating the yarns sold by Reunion Yarn was very labor-intensive. The first—and in some ways, most crucial—step is locating sweaters that work well for unraveling with regard to material, seaming, and design. Emily has become an expert at locating ideal sweaters in thrift stores, but she also receives donations of many unwanted sweaters. After identifying good

candidates, the next steps are to take apart the sweater at the seams, then unravel and wash the yarn. Finally comes the post-processing stage—plying the yarn (industrial machines knit up sweaters with single strands of yarn, not plied yarn). This is where a lot of the fun comes in, because you can create entirely new compositions and colors of yarn when plying.

When the process is complete, there are still some leftover, unusable pieces of yarn—what Emily calls "yarn barf." However, Echoview Fiber Mill in the aptly named town of Weaverville, North Carolina is piloting a process of recycling the chopped up "yarn barf" scraps by mixing them with merino wool before spinning the new yarn, and Emily is excited about the prospect of further reducing waste in the textile process.

At first, Reunion Yarn was a business focused on unraveling unwanted sweaters and reskeining them. But the process was extremely slow and laborious, and with a baby on the way, Emily realized that she couldn't create enough yarn from reskeined sweaters all on her own. "I realized that while I could make an impact recycling the yarn, I could make an even bigger impact teaching people to do it themselves. At fiber festivals, people were always asking, *how do I do this?*" At first, Emily conducted workshops teaching others the process, but then she began developing the concept of an online course that would be accessible to everyone.

"One thing that I learned in the sustainability theory class (at SCAD) was a concept known as enabling solutions, which is also kind of grouped under communities of practice—a group of people practicing and helping each other learn. Enabling is teaching people to take more responsibility for being able to provide for themselves. With the online course, what I'm really trying to do is encourage people to do this themselves, so we have a larger group of people recycling, and that creates a community of practice for textile recycling, which in turn brings even more people into the practice. They see the beauty of the finished yarn."

Emily has already completed a soft launch of her online program, and once she receives feedback and makes the final adjustments, Reunion Yarn's Unraveling Club will be ready for general release. The online program is extremely comprehensive, with start-to-finish instructions broken into six lesson segments, illustrations, videos, written instructions, and an easy-to-follow format that subscribers can view at their own pace. If the launch goes well, Emily is already thinking about adding more online courses on sustainable, textile-related practices.

Emily emphasizes that recycling yarn actually leads to a secondary product that is more beautiful than the original. "Part of my thesis was to show that sustainable products don't have to have this eco-chic aesthetic that we associate with sustainability. I want sustainable stuff but I'm inspired by bright colors, and this is how you can achieve that look. When you're looking at a life cycle analysis, this is more sustainable. I'm not dyeing, I'm not using water. Even if I was using eco-friendly systems to make new yarn, I'm still using up environmental resources to make that yarn. This is truly the most environmental and sustainable way to 'produce' yarn." ⌘

Reunion Yarn

Creator: Emily Felix

Website: www.reunionyarn.com

Instagram: reunionyarn

E-mail: hello@reunionyarn.com

Products: Reskeined yarn in many different weights and fibers, and soon-to-be launched instructional web series with step-by-step lessons to teach others how to reskein

63

Creamsicle Cargo Pouch

by Andrea Hungerford

This pattern is designed to highlight upcycling, by using recycled materials for each part of the cargo pouch. The body is knit from Reunion Yarn, which has been sourced from unraveled sweaters that are then plied and reskeined in new and different color and fiber combinations. The leather is scrap sourced from leftover upholstery pieces, and the canvas lining is linen leftovers from apparel sewing. My goal was to highlight that recycled materials can make as good as – if not better – a finished product as one made with new materials.

One of my favorite shapes for useful bags is the circular pouch, modeled after dry bags or trundle bags. This bag can be opened wide for ease of access, but then pulled tight to ensure that the contents don't spill out. And it's the perfect size and shape for a bottle of wine, a loaf of bread, some cheese, and a tablecloth for an afternoon al fresco picnic!

FINISHED MEASUREMENTS
16" tall and 22" around
Effective length of strap is 25"

MATERIALS
Reunion Yarn Company DK weight (100% cotton, 300 yards). Used double stranded; substitute with the same yardage of another DK weight yarn, or 150 yards of Aran or chunky weight yarn.

Reunion Yarn Company's website explains that they "use minimal electricity and water to unravel second-hand sweaters into beautiful skeins of yarn. We aren't limited by local fibers and natural dyes, allowing you more freedom to use bright colors and a variety of fibers without the guilt of supporting environmentally damaging practices. See the beauty inherent in everything (even an outdated sweater) and understand what it means to find a deeper understanding of the world around you. When you buy a skein of REUNION yarn and make it into something new, you add to the beauty of the material and keep the cycle going!"

Suede leather — scraps can be purchased at upholstery stores or in various Etsy shops (I got mine at www. peggysuealso.com). You can use variously sized scrap pieces, or one piece approx. 36" long and 12" wide

¾ yard of 44" wide sturdy linen or canvas for lining (I used Purl Soho's Warsa Linen in Ecru)

¾ yard of 20" wide medium weight fusible interfacing (I used Pellon Craft Fuse 808(R))

NOTIONS
US 6 (4 mm) 16" circular knitting needle or set of double pointed needles
Stitch marker
Leather sewing machine needle
Thread to match suede and lining fabric
Leather hand sewing needle (optional; needed in the event your sewing machine can't cope with several layers of suede)
Embroidery thread to match suede (optional)

DIRECTIONS
KNITTING
Gauge:
16 sts = 4" in stockinette stitch with DK weight yarn held double, or a single strand of Aran or chunky weight yarn. Adjust needle size if necessary to obtain the correct gauge.

Directions:
With short circular needle or set of double pointed needles, cast on 85 stitches. Place marker and join to work in the round. Knit every round until piece measures 10" from cast on. Bind off.

CUTTING
All cutting dimensions include 1/2" seam allowances.

From suede (see diagram):
Base — a circle 7" in diameter
Body — a rectangle 6" tall and 23" wide
Two straps — each 1 1/2" wide and 28" long

From lining:
Base – a circle 6" in diameter
Body – a rectangle 21" tall and 22" wide

From interfacing:
A rectangle 14" tall and 22" wide

SEWING
Notes:
All seam allowances are ½" unless otherwise specified.
Always use the leather needle(s) when stitching the suede.
Avoid using pins when sewing suede. Use clips such as small binder clamps to hold pieces together temporarily.
Always use a pressing cloth when ironing suede.

1. Assemble the suede pieces.
a) Sew suede body to suede base, leaving 1/2" of the body free at the beginning and end of the circle (for seaming later). Go slow and careful when stitching through the suede—instead of pinning the pieces together, it works better to just slowly ease them together as you constantly turn the pieces to stitch in a circle. Don't worry if there is more than ½" excess at the beginning and end—this can be trimmed if necessary.

b) Sew up the side seam of body, making sure that you stop your stitching right at the point where the body pieces meet the circle. Trim side seam to ½" and press open.

2. Attach the knit piece to the suede piece.
a) With suede piece still inside out, put knit piece inside suede piece so that the right sides of the two pieces are facing each other. Line up the top edges and clip in place

66

with binder clamps, making sure that the knit piece is evenly distributed around. Stitch.

b) Pull knit piece out and press seam down toward the suede piece. Turn right side out and press seam again from the right side.

3. Prepare the lining.
a) Fuse the interfacing to the wrong side of the lining body, aligning bottom edges.

b) Sew lining body to lining base as you did the suede.

c) Sew lining side seam. Trim to 1/2" and press open.

d) Keeping the lining piece inside out, fold the top edge down 4 1/2" and press. Baste 1/4" away from the raw edge.

e) Stitch around the lining 1/2" away from the top fold, to create a channel for the drawstring.

When complete, the lining should appear as in Figure 1.

4. Make and attach strap.
a) Sew the strap by stitching the two strap pieces together along the long sides, with wrong sides together (so that right sides are facing out). Stitch 1/8" away from the edge. When complete, trim the two short sides to create a nice, clean edge, then stitch 1/8" away from each short edge.

b) Position one short edge of the strap over the suede side seam, immediately above the seam where the suede body joins the base. Position the strap so that the short edge is approx. 2" up from the bottom seam, and the strap folds up and over the tab you're stitching down (Figure 2). Stitch down the tab by creating a 1 1/4" box – all four sides and then criss-cross diagonal lines through the box. It can be very difficult stitching the first tab in place, because you'll be stitching through several layers of suede. If this proves too much for your machine, use the leather hand stitch needle and embroidery thread to stitch in place. You can do this with the other end of the strap as well, if you'd like.

c) Position the other short edge of the strap approx. 2" down from the top of the knit piece. Again, position so that the strap folds up and over the tab you're stitching down (Figure 2). Stitch in place as you did the first tab.

5. Attach lining to outer bag.
a) Place lining inside suede/knit outer, so that the wrong sides of both pieces are facing each other. Pull up suede/knit piece so that it isn't slouched or wrinkled, and pin knit and lining pieces together (Figure 3a). The pieces should be positioned so that the line of basting on the lining is hidden under the knit piece, and you should have about 1 1/2" of lining visible above the top edge of the knit/suede piece.

b) Stitch all the way around, 1/2" down from the top edge of the knit piece (Figure 3a). The top of the knitting will roll down neatly and just cover your stitching (Figure 3b). Remove basting from lining.

6. Finishing touches.
a) Stitch through the top tab of the strap again, so that it is sewn into the lining as well as the knit piece —this will give it more stability and keep it from ripping out.

b) Using a seam ripper, pull out just a few stitches at the top of the lining's side seam, then use a safety pin to thread through a drawstring. I used a double strand of the same yarn as the knit body, and then made small tassels for the ends. You will want to knot the ends if you don't add tassels, to make sure that they don't get pulled into the drawstring channel.

Suede Cutting Layout

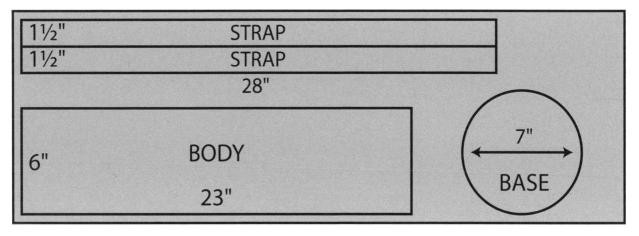

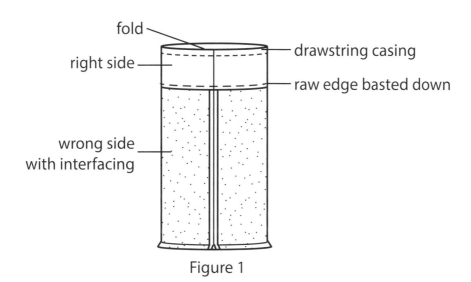

fold

right side

drawstring casing

raw edge basted down

wrong side
with interfacing

Figure 1

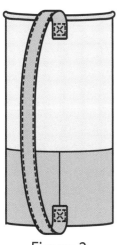

Figure 2

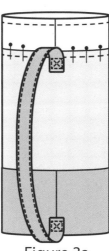

Figure 3a

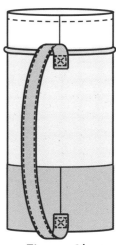

Figure 3b

Radnor Lake Cowl

by Sloane Rosenthal

FINISHED MEASUREMENTS
Width 9.75"
Circumference 36.5"

MATERIALS
Nutmeg Fibers Retreat (70% USA-grown alpaca, 30% USA-grown merino wool; 200 yds / 183 m per 100 g skein)
1 skein in Quebracho & Walnut

US 7 (4.5 mm) straight needles
Yarn needle, waste yarn and US G (4 mm) crochet hook for provisional cast on (optional), spare needle for three-needle bind off (optional)

GAUGE
19 sts and 23 rows = 4" in stockinette stitch and checkerboard mesh stitch, blocked
Gauge is not critical to this project, but may affect finished size and amount of yarn used.

NOTES
Cowl begins with a provisional cast on. After knitting is complete and the piece is blocked, the provisional cast on is undone, the live stitches placed on a needle, and the two ends of the cowl are joined with Kitchener stitch or a three-needle bind off. Alternatively, you may use a regular cast on and join the two ends with a seam.

Always slip the first stitch of every row purlwise with yarn in front.

Checkerboard Mesh Stitch (multiple of 10 sts + 6)
Row 1 (RS): Sl 1, k1, *k3, yo, ssk, k1, [k2tog, yo] 2 times; rep from * to last 4 sts, k4.
Row 2 and all WS rows: Sl 1, purl to last st, k1.
Row 3: Sl 1, k1, *k2, [yo, ssk] 2 times, k1, k2tog, yo, k1; rep from * to last 4 sts, k4.
Row 5: Sl 1, k1, *k1, [yo, ssk] 3 times, k3; rep from * to last 4 sts, k4.
Row 7: Sl 1, k1, *[yo, ssk] 4 times, k2; rep from * to last 4 sts, k4.
Row 9: Sl 1, k1, *k1, [yo, ssk] 3 times, k3; rep from * to last 4 sts, k4.
Row 11: Sl 1, k1, *k2, [yo, ssk] 2 times, k1, k2tog, yo, k1; rep from * to last 4 sts, k4.
Row 13: Sl 1, k1, *k3, yo, ssk, k1, [k2tog, yo] 2 times; rep from * to last 4 sts, k4.
Row 15: Sl 1, k2tog, *yo, k4, [k2tog, yo] 2 times, k2tog; rep from * to last 3 sts, yo, k3.

Row 17: Sl 1, k1, *k2tog, yo, k2, [k2tog, yo] 3 times; rep from * to last 4 sts, k2tog, yo, k2.
Row 19: Sl 1, k2tog, *yo, k4, [k2tog, yo] 2 times, k2tog; rep from * to last 3 sts, yo, k3.
Row 20 (WS): Sl 1, purl to last st, k1.
Repeat Rows 1-20 for pattern.

PATTERN
Cast on: Use a provisional method to CO 46 sts. (Instructions for a crochet provisional cast on can be found at the end of this pattern, or use your preferred method.) Work a set-up row as follows (WS): Sl 1, purl to last st, k1.
OR
Use the long-tail or other stretchy method to CO 46 sts.

Work pattern:
Slipping the first stitch of every row (see Notes) and beginning with a RS row, work in stockinette stitch for 40 rows.

Work Rows 1-20 of checkerboard mesh stitch 2 times (40 rows total).

Work in stockinette stitch for 60 rows.

Work Rows 1-20 of checkerboard mesh stitch 3 times (60 rows total).

Work in stockinette stitch for 10 rows.

End:
If you began with a provisional cast on, place sts on waste yarn. If you began with a regular cast on, loosely BO all sts.

FINISHING
Wet block cowl, using pins and/or blocking wires to open up the lace.

If you began with a provisional cast on, place the live sts

back on the needle, then remove waste yarn from CO edge and place the resulting 46 sts on another needle. Graft (Kitchener stitch) the ends together, or hold with right sides facing and join with a three-needle bind off.

If you began with a regular cast on, seam the two ends of the cowl together.

Steam-block the join and weave in ends.

ABBREVIATIONS

BO	bind off/bound-off	CO	cast on/cast-on
K	knit	K2tog	knit 2 sts together
P	purl	RS	right side
Sl	slip	WS	wrong side
Ssk	[slip 1 as if to knit] 2 times, insert left needle into fronts of these sts and knit them together		
Yo	yarn over		

Checkerboard Mesh Stitch

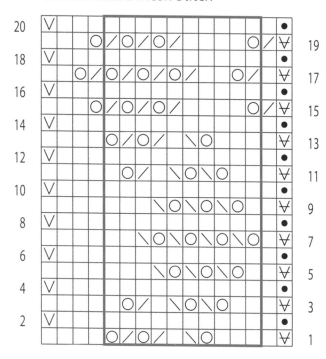

TECHNIQUES

Crochet Provisional Cast On

With waste yarn, make a slip knot loop on the crochet hook. Holding the knitting needle in your left hand and crochet hook in your right, bring the yarn behind the needle. *With the crochet hook in front of the needle, wrap the yarn over the needle and the hook, and pull loop through. 1 st has been cast on the needle. Bring the yarn back between the needle and hook and repeat from * until you have cast on the required number of stitches. Cut yarn and pull tail through last loop to fasten off. To remove the waste yarn later, pick out the fastened-off end and pull the tail to unravel the chain.

Three-Needle Bind Off

Have the two pieces to be joined on separate needles held together in the left hand. Using a third needle, insert into first st on front needle, then first st on back needle and knit them together. *Insert into next st on front needle, then next st on back needle and knit them together, then pass first st on right needle over second to BO 1 st. Repeat from *.

Natural Dyes: Nutmeg Yarn

Nutmeg Yarns is housed in a picture-perfect cedar shed located in Meg Anderson's backyard—just the right size for a few industrial dye pots and rows and rows of newly dyed and yet-to-be-dyed skeins of yarn. Meg's foray into dyeing is rooted in her love of cooking. She began as a bit of kitchen experimentation, making dyes from cabbage, pokeweed, and whatever else she could find to throw into the dye pot. Her home-made dyes quickly evolved into a thriving business, and now 100% of her colors are created by natural dyes derived from plants like pokeweed, madder root, and logwood.

Meg pays attention not only to the source of her dyes, but to how and where her yarn is sourced, as well. All of the wool and alpaca that goes into her yarns is American-raised, and she is in the process of transition-ing her milling to the ecologically focused Echoview Fiber Mill in North Carolina, only a few hours away. Recently, she has begun development on even more local sourcing by creating a line of local farm fibers. Her first batch was 30% Tennessee wool, blended with 70% American me-rino, and the second batch will be 100% Tennessee wool. "I've gotten to know a lot of the farms that have come to fiber festivals as vendors. In this way, I was able to meet some awesome people who were really excited about what I was trying to do," she says. "I started with just one farm, then the next yarn batch included alpaca from two farms, and the next batch will source from four to five local farms."

Nutmeg Yarn

Website:
www.nutmegster.com

Instagram: nutmegfibers

E-mail: info@nutmegster.com

Yarn Lines: lace to bulky
weight, including Farm Fibers,
Squish, Hearth, Homestead,
Trail, Cabin, Retreat, Vale

Teaching: Summer 2017
workshops on natural dyeing
techniques

Nutmeg recently produced its first collection of patterns, as well, published in the Winter 2017 zine. The collection includes five knitting patterns and three recipes. "I love to cook as much as I love to knit, and cooking and knitting seem to go together. Having friends over, having coffee and knitting and eating together . . . I think of knitting and making yarn as a way to share my love of that with other people. I love dyeing the yarn and then you get to take it and do something you love. I think of it the same way with food. I love to make it so that I can share it with others."

Nutmeg currently produces six bases, and Meg's favorites are the "big, squishy, cozy stuff. Chunky weight is easy to learn on and quick to work up, and it shows off texture beautifully. I also want it to be affordable, so that you can actually buy enough to make a whole sweater."

New plans are in the works for Nutmeg Yarns. In addition to further lines of Tennessee-sourced yarn, Meg has summer and fall zines planned, with more new original patterns and recipes. She hopes to increase her focus on pattern design, as well as collaborate with other designers on subsequent books, and keep developing her dye knowledge. This spring, she and her son are planning garden plots for dye plants so that she can grow, harvest, and use her dyes all within her own backyard. ⌘

May Day Bouquet Wrap

by Andrea Hungerford

This past winter, I took advantage of down time in the garden to plan for spring planting, and I decided that I wanted to grow more cut flowers – particularly annuals. One thing I love about growing flowers is that you have a built-in handmade gift right in your backyard. I can't count the number of times that I've realized at the last minute that I need a housewarming gift, or something to take to a sick friend, or a way to say thank-you to one of my daughter's teachers. Being able to run into the backyard, cut some blooms, and immediately have a fresh and beautiful gift that the recipient will always welcome and enjoy is wonderful.

However, I seem to always end up delivering my fresh blooms in a less-than-graceful manner – wrapped in newspaper, or tied up in a plastic bag with a few inches or water. I wanted a simple but elegant wrap for my flowers that added to – rather than detracted from – their beauty.

This bouquet wrap can be made quickly and easily; I make several at a time, so that I always have one available at a moment's notice. The shape is designed to provide a support for the flower heads at the back of the cone, with a lower front edge to show off the blooms to their best advantage. The bottom, pointed end of the cone is watertight and has space to accommodate a small baggie of water rubber-banded to the flower stems to keep them fresh without having water leak everywhere.

You can use a wide variety of materials – I particularly like using something a little more rustic, like traditional linen, on the outside, and something soft and beautiful on the inside. While you can purchase laminated fabrics for the inside lining, it is just as easy to create your own laminated fabric, and this gives you endless options for color and style.

MATERIALS
½ yard outer fabric (I used Door Mill Traditional Linen)
½ yard inner fabric (I used Watercolor Linen and Warsa Linen)
½ yard Heat ‹n Bond Iron-On Vinyl (or any brand of clear iron-on vinyl)
3/4 yard of ribbon, ready made bias tape, or homemade bias tape from lightweight fabrics like cotton lawn, for trim
Matching thread

Depending on the width of your fabrics, you can cut 2–3 wraps from one half-yard piece. However, the vinyl is only 17" wide, so about half a yard will be required for each wrap.

Both the outer and inner fabrics were sourced from Purl So-ho—a wonderful store for makers, available both in-store and online, with a wide variety of different fabric options. The iron-on vinyl is available in many craft stores, as well as online at Amazon.

DIRECTIONS:
1. Create your template
On a piece of paper, draw a circle 15 1/2" in diameter and cut it out. Fold in quarters, then unfold. Mark on the right side of the circle where the crosswise fold intersects the perimeter, then connect with a diagonal line to the bottom of the circle where the lengthwise fold intersects the perimeter. Repeat on the left side. Cut on the diagonal lines, so that you cut off two sides of the circle (see illustration). This is your template. If you like, you can trace it onto a piece of cardboard or quilter's plastic.

2. Cut out your fabrics
Trace the template onto the outer fabric, the inner fabric, and the iron-on vinyl, and cut out one of each.

3. Create your laminated fabric
Following the package directions, iron on the vinyl to the right side of the inner fabric.

4. Sew the pieces together

Pin the inner and outer pieces together, right sides facing. Stitch around the edge with a ½" seam allowance, leaving a 3" opening in the middle of one of the straight sides for turning. Turn right side out. Carefully use a chopstick or another blunt tool to poke out all of the edges and to get a crisp line along the top edge. Push the pointed bottom of the cone as firmly as possible, but don't worry about getting it pushed all the way to the end—having the tip of the cone remain folded up somewhat on the inside gives a less pronounced point to the wrap when closed, and creates a receptacle for a baggie of water rubber-banded around flower stems.

5. Press carefully

Press all of the edges to get a crisp line, being careful not to touch the hot iron to the vinyl side of the fabric (or put the paper backing from the vinyl over the laminated fabric for protection, and then go ahead and press). Turn in the edges of the 3" opening, press them in place, and pin.

6. Sew on your trim

You can experiment with different types of trim – for one of my samples, I sewed several lengths of ribbon into the side seam (see next step). For the other samples, I created bias tape from Liberty of London lawns and other lightweight fabrics, pinned the bias tape along the top curved edge, and stitched it close to the edge of the tape (making sure to catch the tape on both the front and the back in the stitching).

7. Sew the side seam

Fold the wrap in half, right sides together, and sew the side seam with a 1/2" seam allowance, making sure to backstitch at beginning and end. This will close up the 3" opening you left for turning. Protecting the vinyl with paper, press the seam open.

8. Optional ribbon

You can use ready-made ribbon, or create a length of ribbon from leftover fabric or bias tape that matches the trim. The wrap does not need a ribbon tie in order to securely hold a bouquet, but it is a beautiful finishing touch!

80

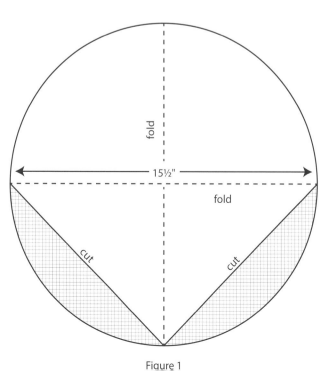

fold

15½"

fold

cut

cut

Figure 1

Karen Templer's concept for Fringe Association is a place for makers—particularly knitters—to find good content, in both community dialogue and quality supplies for hand making. Fringe Association's online store is based on things that Karen herself likes to use: quality-made bags, needles, and notions. "I have to honestly be able to say that it's something that I would want to buy before I decide to stock it."

But Fringe Association also provides content in the form of a community that opens up a wide variety of topics for online discussion between knitters and makers around the world, propelled by Karen's daily blog, which she describes as "a style blog from a handmade perspective." Sometimes those discussions are practical in nature, such as tutorials for specific knitting skills. Other times, those discussions are complex and multi-layered; for instance, issues related to slow fashion, how to build a wardrobe comprised only of clothing that you love and use regularly, and how to combat a society that often appears to value material goods—and lots of them—above concepts like sustainability and simplicity.

"My interest in slow fashion developed very organically," Karen explains. "I have always sewed since the time I was a kid, off and on. Learning to knit really brought me back to what it was like to make clothes ... I was thinking about making what I want and not being dependent on what's available in the stores." Karen says that when she moved from the Bay Area to Nashville several years ago, it gave her the opportunity to put these thoughts into action and to get rid of everything but those pieces of clothing that she really loved and actually wore. "This got me thinking about slow fashion,

about being really mindful. I want to try to make as much of my wardrobe as I can, and I started becoming conscious about where the raw materials for making are coming from."

When Karen discusses potentially controversial issues on her blog, it can cause emotions to run high, and readers have a wide variety of responses. But providing a forum for such discussions raises readers' awareness levels of these issues and gives them a chance to exchange ideas and expose each other to new information and perspectives.

"For me, it's always ultimately about leading people to the good stuff—helping people make good decisions about materials, or providing them with a quality option . . . I want to give people the tools to make choices for themselves. One of my goals is to figure out what are the choices you can make, and how to make those choices."

Some of Fringe Association's most popular posts are how-to tutorials and knit-alongs that encourage participants to create their own garments. Karen says that "the thing I enjoy most is empowering people. They can make choices and make changes. The beauty of making your own clothes is that you can adapt them. Patterns have to be standardized, but if you have the know-how, you can change them." ⌘

Fringe Association

Creator: Karen Templer

Website:
www.fringeassociation.com

Shop: www.fringesupplyco.com

Instagram: karentempler

Content: daily blog

Shop: Knitting accessories, including project bags, needles, scissors, notions, pouches

Iconic downtown Nashville scenes: even on a Wednesday night you'll find a musician playing saxophone in the middle of Broadway (top left); the landmark Acme Feed & Seed, long gone but now preserved as street art (bottom left); and just one example of the larger than life representation of the cowboy boots signs, murals, and stores that you see everywhere (bottom right).

Slow Knitting: Hannah Thiessen

When Hannah Thiessen was eight years old and living in rural Kentucky, one of the local church constituents invited her and five other children to her home—an old renovated barn—after church on Sundays to learn how to knit. She taught the kids to make their own knitting needles out of dowels and clay, and then taught them basic knitting stitches. "One by one, the other kids stopped coming, until it was just me." Hannah recalls idyllic moments during those times—baby sheep, cats in the barn rafters, cookie baking—while she continued to learn knitting, as well as rudimentary spinning and yarn dyeing with Kool-Aid.

Years later, Hannah continued to pursue her love of fiber by learning to paint with acrylics and pursuing a degree in textiles fashion. She fulfilled her internship requirement for the degree by living in Uruguay for two months and working for Malabrigo. She helped the company style the photographs for its upcoming pattern book, and subsequently acted as creative director for the next Malabrigo book. She then worked for Premiere Yarns as creative director, and then assisted Shibui Knits and Knit Purl with online newsletters and social media posts. Hannah's working education in the yarn industry continued as she worked with her mom to open a yarn store in Iowa and then helped to start a yarn subscription service called Yarn Box. She next increased her knowledge of social media influence and marketing as a product coordinator for Inked Brands, an influencer commerce company that worked with bloggers to monetize their followings through advertising and products.

All of these experiences helped Hannah to hone her niche in the knitting and yarn industry: social media marketing and creative direction. Hannah now does freelance work for various designers and companies, helping to develop styling, brand development, and marketing.

In the course of this work, Hannah began to brainstorm a concept for a book that focused on "slow knitting." "I've always cared about where wool comes from because that's how I was introduced to it . . . I saw that there was a need for people to really start addressing sourcing in a big way . . . not just the source material (yarn), but the stories about the people who make the yarn and raise the sheep. I was inspired by Clara Parkes' writings, and I wanted to talk about who's raising the sheep and who's making the yarn, and then find designers who would talk about how they match the yarn to their original design and celebrate the yarn through their work. I had met so many wonderful designers—artists and true craftspeople—I wanted to celebrate and support their work."

Hannah wrote her own book proposal and pitched the idea to a publisher, and the project was green-lighted. "A journey from sheep to skein to stitch," is the book's subheading, and Hannah explains the concept as "always embracing the process of your projects." She says that "working on the book has made me live the philosophy." She has significantly reduced her yarn stash, buying only yarn that is really special to her, and she tries to buy American-made wool whenever possible from producers "who can tell me the origins and process of the fiber."

"I want to feel like what I make is who I am—similar to the slow food idea that you are what you eat. I think the struggle with embracing slow fashion is that it is easy to feel overwhelmed. I'm not a minimalist visually. I love color and saturation, which is what led to lots of stashed yarn, because I loved so many colors and wanted to have all of the colors in a collection. I decided this year that instead of feeling like I have to give up my love of color to have a small wardrobe, I'm instead going to focus on my love of print in garments, and the celebration of the quality of the material. When I knit with something, I want to celebrate a small project in a bright color. I'll knit something small that I can give away, so that I can experience the joy of working with a particular yarn or color without accumulating more and more items in my wardrobe." ⌘

Hannah Thiessen

Website: www.handmadebyhannahbelle.com

Ravelry:
www.ravelry.com/designers/hannah-thiessen

Instagram: hannahbelleknits

"Slow Knitting" is scheduled to release
Oct. 10, 2017

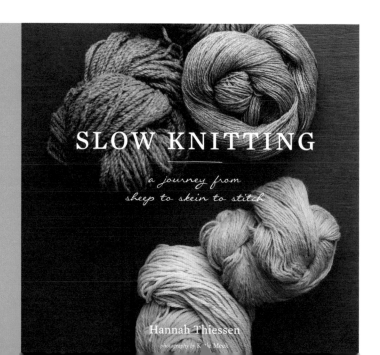

SLOW KNITTING

*a journey from
sheep to skein to stitch*

Hannah Thiessen
photography by Kate Meek

Hannah's home is a cozy nook with an extensive library of knitting reference materials and coffee table books, a carefully curated stash of favorite yarn brands and her own handspun yarn, a well-used and much-loved hand crocheted afghan that showcases Hannah's love of color, and housecats Thusa and Leo (pictured at right).

By Hand Author and Photographer

Andrea Hungerford is an obsessive knitter who lives with her husband, three daughters and three cats, a Great Pyrenees farm dog, and a variety of chickens on acreage outside of Portland, Oregon. Andrea's "mini-farm" affords her the opportunity to grow vegetables, berries, fruit trees, and cutting flowers. Andrea has never met a hand craft that doesn't intrigue her, and her current repertoire of making includes sewing, quilting, embroidery, mosaics, hand thrown pottery, canning, candlemaking, photography, and anything involving fiber and fabric. Her heart, however, belongs to knitting, and she can often be found during the summer in a corner of her garden, with her latest knitting project flying off her needles.

Karen DeWitz lives in the woods just outside of Oregon City with her husband, teenage son (whose older brother is away at college), and a rambunctious fluffy dog. Karen was a teacher for ten years and then edited math textbooks for many more before turning full-time to her two great passions: photography and great books. (She kept her amateur status in her other favorite pastimes: hiking and drinking coffee.) She loves to photograph common things in new or evocative ways and is always looking for interesting angles, contrasts of light, or unusual patterns in everyday moments. She spends way more time than she should admit photographing hummingbirds and raindrops in her yard. When she's not taking pictures or chasing after her escape-artist dog, Karen also edits YA and middle grade novels.

Upcoming Issues

Upcoming issues of **By Hand** will feature different makers' communities around the country, including:

- Puget Sound region
- Great Lakes region
- Northern California
- Denver
- British Columbia
- New York
- North Carolina

If you have suggestions for an artist or maker, a knitting store or small business, or anything unique in these locations, we'd love to hear from you! Do you know of a makers' community that you think we should profile? If so, let us know! Email us at: info@byhandserial.com.

You can also find us on:
Ravelry at www.ravelry.com/groups/by-hand-serial
Facebook at www.facebook.com/byhandserial
Instagram at www.instagram.com/byhandserial